INSIDER INVESTING
FOR REAL
ESTATE AGENTS

 W9-BYJ-471

INSIDER INVESTING FOR REAL ESTATE AGENTS

How to Profit from Your Intimate Knowledge of the Market

WALTER S. SANFORD

WILEY

John Wiley & Sons, Inc.

Copyright © 2006 by Sanford Systems. All rights reserved.

Published by John Wiley & Sons, Inc., Hoboken, New Jersey.
Published simultaneously in Canada.

No part of this publication may be reproduced, stored in a retrieval system, or transmitted in any form or by any means, electronic, mechanical, photocopying, recording, scanning, or otherwise, except as permitted under Section 107 or 108 of the 1976 United States Copyright Act, without either the prior written permission of the Publisher, or authorization through payment of the appropriate per-copy fee to the Copyright Clearance Center, Inc., 222 Rosewood Drive, Danvers, MA 01923, (978) 750-8400, fax (978) 646-8600, or on the web at www.copyright.com. Requests to the Publisher for permission should be addressed to the Permissions Department, John Wiley & Sons, Inc., 111 River Street, Hoboken, NJ 07030, (201) 748-6011, fax (201) 748-6008, or online at http://www.wiley.com/go/permissions.

Limit of Liability/Disclaimer of Warranty: While the publisher and author have used their best efforts in preparing this book, they make no representations or warranties with respect to the accuracy or completeness of the contents of this book and specifically disclaim any implied warranties of merchantability or fitness for a particular purpose. No warranty may be created or extended by sales representatives or written sales materials. The advice and strategies contained herein may not be suitable for your situation. You should consult with a professional where appropriate. Neither the publisher nor author shall be liable for any loss of profit or any other commercial damages, including but not limited to special, incidental, consequential, or other damages.

For general information on our other products and services or for technical support, please contact our Customer Care Department within the United States at (800) 762-2974, outside the United States at (317) 572-3993 or fax (317) 572-4002.

Wiley also publishes its books in a variety of electronic formats. Some content that appears in print may not be available in electronic books. For more information about Wiley products, visit our web site at www.wiley.com.

The purchaser of Walter Sanford's *Insider Investing for Real Estate Agents* is hereby authorized to use all systems contained in this work subject to broker and legal counsel for the purchaser's real estate brokerage and investing business. Purchaser is to use the concepts in this system for the purpose for which they are intended and to reproduce the forms for such purpose. Such reproduction requires no further permission from the author, publisher, and/or payment of any permission fee.

The reproduction of any form for sale, for incorporation in any publication intended for sale, for use in training programs, or for the insertion in any publication (whether print or digital) is *prohibited* without the permission of and credit to the author and publisher: Sanford Systems and Strategies, 559 South Washington Avenue, Kankakee, IL 60901.

Library of Congress Cataloging-in-Publication Data:

Sanford, Walter S., 1956-
    Insider investing for real estate agents : how to profit from
your intimate knowledge of the market / Walter S. Sanford.
       p.   cm.
    ISBN-13: 978-0-471-98862-5 (pbk.)
    ISBN-10: 0-471-98862-6 (pbk.)
    1. Real estate agents.   2. Real estate investment.   3. Real
estate business.   I. Title.
    HD1382.S26   2006
    332.63'24—dc22
                                                    2006008110

Printed in the United States of America.

10 9 8 7 6 5 4 3 2 1

To all the real estate agents
who have seen me go down . . .
and up in the past 30 years
and also to my beautiful wife and children
who appreciate that I paid attention
to these lessons.

CONTENTS

When I first started investing, I never dreamed that I would become a real estate broker. When I became a real estate broker, I never dreamed that my investing experience and activities would help me so much in my new brokerage business.

As my experience and skill level grew over the years, the two businesses, which were distinctly different yet used the same tools, became intertwined to the point where each investment contained aspects of my brokerage business and each brokerage transaction was a potential investment.

Real estate brokers and agents are going to be pleasantly surprised and excited to learn the strategies in this book. Whether it is to find buyers from among your tenants or inventory from your sellers, working both businesses at the same time, ethically and honestly, has the potential for greatly increasing your income.

Many times in my real estate brokerage career, I relied on the gains made through my investing activities to fight the burnout from consistently jumping through hoops for my clients. The businesses are complementary and extremely profitable using the conservative methods presented in this book.

As a real estate broker or agent, you are going to find that meeting the demands of your position is just like holding a seat on the stock exchange. You are at ground zero tracking your inventory and negotiating with buyers and tenants through the relationships that you foster on both sides of these two great businesses.

I have been one of the top real estate trainers in the country for the past 10 years, and I was one of the top real estate agents in North America during the 1980s and 1990s. Over time, my company has developed numerous systems that allow you to duplicate the systems that many top agents have used with great success. The systems in this book will allow *you* to achieve the dreams you have for you and your family—they did for me!

INSIDER INVESTING
FOR REAL
ESTATE AGENTS

CHAPTER I

The Insider's Buckets

Make no mistake—this is not a manual on how to steal real estate with no money down. I have thought out and proven every aspect of this book during my years of experience as an agent/investor and through hundreds of interviews with agents who enjoy living off their investments. Their stories are always the same: They ran an outstanding real estate business that produced huge amounts of net income. At the same time, they invested in the asset that they know best—real estate. In the later years, they have left energy-zapping tasks of real estate sales to younger and more active agents and have been able to pick and choose the aspects of the business that they enjoy the most. Soon, their real estate rental income will replace commission income, and some of these agents will open management companies that have evolved from the management of their own properties. Some will become speakers. All of them can retire as financially independent real estate agents/brokers with positive cash flow.

As you read this book, you will learn how to make many decisions: Where will your seed money come from? Will you invest for appreciation or cash flow? Will you be a speculator or a business owner? Your answers will show you exactly where you need to invest and when you need to invest. *Where* has a lot to do with risk aversion, and *when* will be compounded by where you are today in terms of the market, your available funds for down payments, and whether you have already filled what I call *bucket one* necessities of life.

Bucket one investments include your business insurance, tax-deferred retirement accounts such as Simplified Employment Pensions (SEPs), Individual Retirement Accounts (IRAs), Keoghs, Roths, savings accounts, improvements to your business that ensure future cash flow growth, and the holding of nonsecured debt to absolute minimums. You should accomplish the real estate investments discussed in this book *after* you have started and partially funded bucket one investments.

Real estate is a *bucket two* investment, and because you are a real estate professional, it is where your insider insights are most likely to lead you. It only makes sense that as a wholesale purveyor of the world's greatest investment product, you should choose investments where you have the greatest knowledge and the best chance of success.

Bucket three items might include a second home, appreciating collectibles, or the setting up of an annuity for foundations, charities, or your family. It is important to know where you are in life. Bucket one, which represents your financial foundation, needs to be adequate and safe before you invest in real estate. You should pay off all nonsecured high interest rate debt, have six months' earnings in the bank, and have insurance in place (life, medical, and disability). Your source of income must be secure and growing, and all tax-leveraged investments should be maxed out before you consider investing in real estate. To provide this foundation, establish your real estate business before you move to the riskier buckets.

This book is all about finding unprecedented success by using the advantage of your insider abilities to garner a substantial real estate portfolio. I describe the systems and strategies that I developed to gain the majority of market share in my region and have included the advice that I have found most useful when coaching real estate agents.

The system I describe in this book is about investing within the business plan of your real estate career and determining whether you are ready to blend the two.

Although this is not a book about real estate speculation, you can use speculation if appropriate. The real estate professional has many advantages over the average investor, and this book highlights and incorporates them. Your real estate brokerage business, real estate investing business, and most important, your net worth are about to change . . . for the positive!

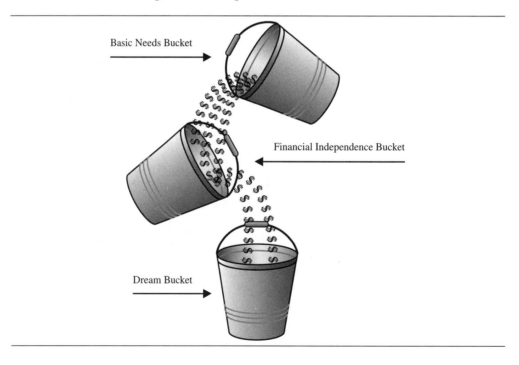

Basic Needs Bucket

Financial Independence Bucket

Dream Bucket

CHAPTER 2

How I Became a Real Estate Agent and an Insider Real Estate Investor

Many times real estate agents who have been successful in brokering real estate transactions find a property that meets some real or perceived investment need. They purchase that property, allowing their real estate business to lead them into real estate investment. My experience was flipped. I first became a real estate investor, based on a windfall of money that came to me, then became a real estate broker after I lost it all.

Winning a lottery when I was 16 years old allowed me to begin my investing career. In the western states, the government initiated a lottery called the "Simultaneous Oil and Gas Lease Drawings." These drawings, which were prevalent in the early 1970s, gave people the opportunity to pay $20 for a chance to own an oil and gas lease that might or might not be valuable.

Thirty years ago, it was hard for a 16-year-old to come by $20. I mowed a few lawns, and I borrowed $10 from my dad. I mailed in my $20 ticket fee. Being 16, I promptly forgot about the lottery as more pressing matters (cars, girls . . . what else was there?) took precedence.

Approximately four months later, a man showed up at our home unannounced, saying that I had won a 10-year lease in Campbell County, Wyoming, and that he wanted to talk to my father about negotiating a purchase. This man had a $10,000 check with him to buy the lease that night. My father, being one of the world's greatest negotiators, said that if someone flew unannounced from New Mexico to make an unsolicited offer, maybe that offer could be bettered. He promptly asked the man if we could get back to him.

My father researched the oil and gas leases surrounding my winning piece of ground; he contacted the owners of those properties near mine. He negotiated the sale to the Atlantic Richfield Oil Corporation (ARCO), which held other leases in the area. ARCO gave us $36,000 for the rights to this oil and gas lease. My father also negotiated a percentage of any oil and gas found on the property over the next 10 years.

My 16-year-old response to all this excitement was versed in the classic vernacular of the 1970s, "COOL!" I could see my car—a Porsche, of course. I could see myself driving down the coolest of all college campuses and attracting the most beautiful coeds.

My hopes were diminished when my father, who had loaned me $10 of the $20 initial investment, mentioned his ownership rights to the lease, thus cutting my proceeds from $36,000 to $18,000. But in the 1970s, you could still get an excellent used "914" for $18,000. I presented this game plan to my father. His response—"You need money for your future, seed capital for business, and a savings account for college!" I felt nauseous.

I explained how necessary it was to have a car. He calmed my anxieties and said that he had not forgotten about buying a car for me. His priority, however, was to obtain a growth vehicle for our money, and real estate was said to be a fast-moving investment.

A family friend and real estate broker helped us find a fourplex in El Monte, California. On seeing the fourplex, my father explained that I would be the new manager for this property and would be learning tricks of the trade as an owner. This sounded all too boring to me, and none of it included the part where I got my car.

From the proceeds, my dad graciously held out $400 for my first car. This allowed me to get a used Mazda—it was *not* a chick magnet. I made the best of it with my father's advice: He told me to drive the young coeds by the fourplex. He said that if I pointed out the potential for appreciation, then they would understand my investment prowess and income prospects. This would help me achieve great success with girls and life.

During this period, listings were scarce. An agent caught me on the front lawn of my new building. We listed the fourplex and received offers almost immediately. We took the best and sold it. At the closing, I realized that I had more than doubled my money. When I inquired how this could happen so fast, our real estate agent said, "This always happens! Real estate is an amazing investment." I had to agree because the balance in my savings account proved it.

A 12-unit property was available down the street from the original fourplex. Based on my almost superhuman abilities as a real estate investor, we negotiated, purchased it, and within months, had a buyer who wanted it much more than we did. This time we tripled our down payment investment.

Our next purchase was a 91-unit property in downtown Los Angeles. Once again, the miraculous quick turn of a hot Southern California market left my savings account brimming over.

I realized that I now knew everything there was to know about real estate and did not need my father's advice in investing or his constant nagging to slow down. So, I nicely bought out Dad and started investing my own money. My first investment went to a new, European delivery Turbo Porsche Carrera direct from Stuttgart, Germany. This supercar was a premature bucket three investment. The day that it arrived, I showed it off to everyone by parking it at my new college fraternity house, Kappa Alpha, at the University of Southern California. There was no one bigger than me!

Anything that I bought in real estate seemed to turn to gold. I had advanced my empire to include Arizona, Washington, and other states. Since real estate continued to go up unabated, I foolishly bought properties without even looking at them and cleared them of tenants because I believed that it was the only way to properly repair a building. Then I hired workers to paint and renovate these acquisitions so I could generate higher incomes, thus higher sales prices. Negative cash flow did not concern me because of high appreciation rates and the quick turn, short holding periods.

Then Came 1979 . . .

Mortgage rates that reached 18 percent changed my real estate world. I was caught with many vacant apartment buildings in numerous states. I had brokers telling me that the equity I had expected to receive was not available; in fact, some of the properties were actually worth less than the high-leverage loans that I had on them. Losing a property in foreclosure or selling in a distressed market is one of the worst experiences that a real estate investor can ever have. I graduated from USC with a degree in real estate finance and a life lesson in real estate speculation.

I decided it was time to apologize to my father for my past arrogance and once again seek his advice. My father thought that I was young and smart and could reach the top again; however, neither of us yet realized that when you lose everything, you can actually go way past zero.

To pay my debts, I had to earn a huge sum of money each month *before* I could even buy groceries. I had no seed capital and only a checkered past of real estate experience. I asked my dad what kind of job could help me make enough money to get out of trouble. He suggested real estate sales would be good for me. He said that since I had lost more money than most people make in a lifetime, my background would probably provide a valuable frame of reference to anyone I represented. It made sense to me. With my experience, I would have a leg up on the competition.

I went to Long Beach, California, to start my new career. One of my unsold real estate investments was in Long Beach, and I could actually move into it. The property was a large California mission style home that had been built in the 1930s and had not been upgraded since World War II; it needed a ton of work before it would be acceptable to my new wife, who was used to my *mucho dinero* days. The only way to get enough money to refurbish the home and pay off my huge debt was to become a very successful real estate agent.

Once again, my dad intervened with some sage advice: "You can become anyone you want to be by just doing what they did." Keeping that in mind, I took many real estate agents out to lunch and arranged meetings with the top agents from all over the United States and Canada. From the information they provided, I learned how to become a successful real estate agent and a top producer.

At this point in my life, I learned that earning real estate commissions is a business that requires attention every day. I based my real estate systems around proactive seller lead generation systems that helped me get a larger percentage of listings in my neighborhood. Once I had the listing leads, I developed a better listing presentation to gain a larger percentage of signatures on listing contracts at the correct price. This allowed me to put up a larger percentage of signs, which created more buyer phone calls. With systems in place to eliminate unprofitable buyers and to work only with profitable buyers, I found that I could close transactions in less time than a majority of my competitors.

Good systems and checklists, coupled with monitoring by an assistant, allowed me to "duplicate" myself and delegate responsibilities that I was not excited about doing. This enabled me to better utilize my affiliates in teams and free up more time to conduct proactive seller lead generation. As a single-man office, I could achieve the production level of most full offices and still find time to seek investments.

While earning money as a real estate broker, I was viewing the best inventory for free. As I created proactive seller lead generation, I could find off-market inventory that was available to purchase for myself. The only problem was finding the down payment.

CHAPTER 3

Insiders Have a Down Payment Machine

This chapter presents one of the elements in my real estate investment system that is most controversial because it is unlike what a lot of real estate gurus teach: I believe it is paramount for an insider real estate investor (a real estate agent) to have a savings account and a down payment prior to investing in real estate. Your *down payment machine*—your successful real estate brokerage business—will fund this account. If you try to skip this first step, you will have to borrow money, bring in an investor, or find one of those extremely rare "no money down" transactions with the potential problems described later in this chapter. Without a down payment, it will be much harder for you to find the diamond of real estate investing: a *performing property* with a positive cash flow.

Although having a property perform correctly with little or no money out of pocket is every investor's dream, it is improbable that you will obtain such a piece of real estate. In my 30 years' experience, I have found that when the down payment is minimum or nonexistent, the insider investor usually gives up some attribute of a performing piece of real estate: location, condition, a positive or break-even cash flow, the potential for future appreciation, safe financial terms, or possibly control over the investment.

Obviously, location has a lot to do with any real estate investment. It determines not only how easy it will be for you to collect rents (you should not need a gun to collect rent!), but also how well you can maintain the quality of your tenants and the rate of future appreciation.

Condition will affect your future cash flow. You will need to address deferred maintenance needs and major problems with any of your systems during your ownership.

A positive or break-even cash flow is critical because it gives you holding power. Since the millennium, many investors have found that investing for speculation and trying to squeeze the last few dollars of appreciation in an unbelievably hot market can be elusive. Many people missed the top and are still holding on in hopes of a rebound. If it is not forthcoming, then these investors may find it difficult to keep a property with a monthly "alligator" biting them in the rear. Although my system is not based on future appreciation, that possibility always exists when you buy a property in a mediocre-to-good area. It has been proven that appreciation is consistently positive in real estate, but you have to weather those short-term drops before you can take advantage of the next climb in value.

Holding power has a lot to do with the safety of your financial terms. Not only do we like to see low interest rates that lead to the possibility of positive or break-even cash flow, but we also like to see long-term loans that are fully amortized, which will eliminate the need to refinance or sell the property.

Last, and most important, insider investors should have control over their investments. Whenever you bring in a partner, you bring in the potential for pain. Seldom do partners have the same needs and ideas on how to manage, use, and market any piece of real estate. If you are not *married* to the partner, in every sense of the word, avoid partnerships. My experience has been that partnerships breed distrust and disagreements making someone an eventual loser.

The smartest financial move is to have ready cash for real estate transactions that meet all the goals of this book. You might ask, "Why not refinance another piece of property to obtain enough money for a down payment on a rapidly appreciating piece of real estate?" There really is nothing wrong with that as long as real estate keeps appreciating and as long as the piece of property you have refinanced can service the debt and expenses with the income that it produces. However, this strategy ignores one of my goals: *Free and clear property is nice to have when you are old.*

Many of you will say that buying well-performing property and waiting for the tenants to pay off the mortgage is a slow track to investment success. This criticism reminds me of my ex-wife's response when the subject of horrendously high alimony came up—her answer to my pain was "Work harder!" I'm telling you the same thing now. Make more money in your real estate brokerage using my systems and look harder for the best real estate investments.

The strategy of earning your money, investing it correctly, and allowing your tenants to pay off the mortgage is a tried-and-true approach that works in every market. Many real estate agents do not have experience with a sideways or falling market, but as in any business cycle—they happen. I want the readers of this book to know how to weather the good times, the boring times, and even the "where's the bottom?" kinds of markets.

In Southern California between 1980 and 1985, we experienced as much as 15 percent to 30 percent drops in real estate prices from their 1979 highs. From

1990 to 1995, a good percentage of the transactions in Southern California were actually being closed at prices less than the amounts owed the banks on mortgages. We were receiving concessions from the lenders to achieve a closed property and then eventually a commission. This is called a *short pay.* This is a concept where banks that expect to foreclose on property secured by one of their loans will accept a discount on the repayment of their loan, in a sale, as long as it happens before they have to foreclose. These ups and downs happen everywhere (although not as pronounced in some locations). Any investment program based on future appreciation is bound to fail. Owning real estate that can weather the storms and provide equity paydowns through your tenants' rent is one of the safest and—because of a snowball effect—one of the fastest, most exciting roads to real estate wealth.

This whole system is based on your ability to make a 5, 10, or even 25 percent down payment. I am going to give you some ideas for getting this money based on the discipline of earning and keeping money as a real estate professional:

- Master many seller lead generation systems to produce leads no matter how busy you get.
- Learn to determine whether buyers are profitable by their actions and commitment.
- Develop checklists and technology to systemize the steps necessary for success including lead generation, listing presentations, marketing, inventory locating for buyers, negotiating, closing, transaction coordinating, and follow-up. You also must run your business efficiently and maintain a balance in your life while you are doing everything else.

Since obtaining a down payment is essential to your success in real estate investing, you must use your insider advantages to become a better real estate agent, thus creating a higher net profit. A major goal of this book is to show you how to *have your money work for you so you don't have to work so hard for your money in a real estate brokerage.*

It is important to understand that you have chosen a business that requires you to be available to your clients frequently. In fact, your clients expect you to jump through hoops all the time. Sometimes you may find it difficult to take a vacation because you are afraid of missing "that big deal." The burnout ratio for real estate agents, especially top producers, seems to occur between the 10- and 20-year mark of a career. When you wake up and realize that you are not as excited about the brokerage business as you once were, it will be nice if you can fall back on savings and equity in real estate that produce a positive cash flow.

My first big step as an agent came when I moved from comfortable entry level, residential real estate up to higher priced transactions in residential property, thereby working the same amount of time while netting larger commissions. As my client base continued to grow, I transitioned into the investment-oriented and commercial aspects of real estate, a move that was accelerated by my early exposure to investment real estate.

Eventually, I became a mentor to other top agents who recognized that my systems work. While advancing my professional career goals, I slowly built my real estate investments (a second time). This is not to say that I did not make many mistakes in accumulating those real estate investments (which I talk about later), but my constant goal was to have my money work for me so I did not have to work so hard for it. And this time, I was doing it safely.

At this point, I want you to start thinking about how much real estate brokerage business you have to do to save a down payment for buying real estate. To reach this goal, you may need to make improvements in your brokerage business. In addition, there are some expenses you need to consider *before* you set aside money for your down payment and our investment program.

Going back to my bucket theory, there are investments you should make before you buy real estate. I recommend that you contribute fully to your tax-free investment accounts and that you minimize your credit card debt, student loans, or other nonsecured debt.

Form 3.1, at the end of this chapter, provides worksheets that will give you some idea of the minimum goals you should establish. The philosophies underlying these worksheets are based on age-old rules for financial success. If you follow them, you will win. If you do not follow them, you are unlikely to maximize your contributions to family, faith, fun, friends and, of course, personal finances.

Make certain that you have an end date for your "have to" working life and create a time to retire while living off the fruits of your labor from properties you have purchased with your insider advantage. It is an exciting exercise, and you need to give serious thought to the results.

Finding a down payment is one of the most difficult parts of any real estate investment program. Many of my early tax returns showed extremely small net income because in my search to find the keys to the kingdom of real estate sales, I was looking for tax-deductible expenses to add to my Schedule C. I used those expenses to reduce my net income, thereby reducing my taxes. As a result, banks sometimes did not consider my loan applications seriously. I know how it feels when you are starting out and hunting for money to do deals. Early in my career,

I was forced to make compromises to my edicts of 10 percent down and no partners. I can understand if you bring in a client to help you or if you use notes and trust deeds that you had previously taken back as part of your commission. I understand using your commission dollars toward a down payment. In rare cases, where the deal is just an amazing opportunity, I can certainly understand borrowing money from family, friends, or even institutional/hard sources. Getting started can be the hardest part, especially when your real estate net profit income has not kicked in. I have even written one or two no-money-down deals where I did not compromise the other important factors of a real estate investment.

Although it can seem like an insurmountable task, the important thing is simply to get started in your investment career. You have to generate leads for sellers and handle buyers while making enough profit to handle your personal living expenses. But if you make investing part of your goal, some of the properties you struggle to get into will be the crown jewels of your investment portfolio in a few years.

I discovered the magic of equity paydowns through fully amortized loans. This strategy, coupled with the appreciation of real estate and the cash flow of your investment property, can substantially increase your net worth. Whatever your goals may be, make them bright and shiny enough for you to go through this initial pain of scraping together a down payment. Many hot buttons in my life encouraged me to pursue my investment program. My motivations and desires have changed over the years, but they have included the following goals:

- Financial independence and material comfort
- A waterfront home
- Proof of self-worth
- Vacation properties and automobiles
- Proof that others were wrong about my abilities
- Desire to be a local celebrity
- Fear of failure
- Enough money to be a mentor and help others
- Prestige and freedom

To motivate my success, I needed to see a very bright light at the end of the tunnel. Many times you will run into roadblocks. As long as you can anticipate the feeling of accomplishment that you will have when you achieve any of your goals, breaking through barriers will be much easier. Form 3.1 is a planning exercise and will help you find out how to earn the down payments for the real estate that can make your dreams come true.

When you have completed Form 3.1 and know how much cash you will need, you must implement seller lead generation programs to accomplish your seller contact goals. The most effective and least expensive method to obtain buyers and earn commissions is to acquire listings. Having signs up is the cheapest way to find buyers. It is also a great way to find real estate opportunities for personal investment.

Now, make the commitment to the people you love as well as to your broker or manager by filling out the Insider's Performance form on the next page.

The Insider's Performance Commitment

I, _____, being
a committed, self confident, aggressive real estate agent/broker in pursuit of
my real estate investment goal, voluntarily commit to the following:

1. During the next 6 months, I will be my own best client and buy a little of
    what I sell! I will need to get my bucket one investments in shape and
    have enough money to fund my down payment.

2. In the next 12 months, I will earn $ _____.

3. I will obtain _____ # of listings each month.

4. I will go on _____ # of listing appointments each
    week.

5. I will make _____ # of listing contacts each
    week.

6. I will make _____ sales each month.

7. I will show _____ properties each week.

Should I begin to fall behind, I will request that my broker go over my
program, my successes, my setbacks, and my plans to help me stay on
schedule so that I can get myself, my family, and my charities those things
which I have committed to and deserve.

_____   _____
Your Signature   Date

I acknowledge receipt of this commitment. I am also committed to your
success and will monitor your progress.

_____   _____
Your Broker   Date

_____   _____
Walter Sanford   Date
Mentor

Please make five photocopies of this commitment sheet. Give a copy to your
family, your broker, and send one to me!

Bucket One Investments: A Planning Exercise*

You have chosen a career that allows you to choose the type of life you want to live and the level of income that you want or need to achieve. How much cash do you need to fund your bucket one investments; pay off your high interest, short-term, and unsecured debt; get stuff you "have to have"; *and* fund a real estate investment?

Bucket One Investments

1. Cash reserves in money market funds
(six months' net income is acceptable)   _____

2. Disability insurance that, if needed,
will keep your household running
without undue pressure (annual premium)   + _____

3. All tax-leveraged or employer-assisted
retirement accounts (IRA, SEP,
simple, Keogh, Roth, pension)   + _____

4. Other insurance, if needed   + _____

Total Bucket One Investments   _____

Debt Reduction

1. Unsecured debt at rates higher
than current nonconforming
mortgage interest rates   + _____

2. Items I have to contractually
pay off this year   + _____

3. Purchases that are more
important than my real estate
investment program

   _____ + _____

   _____ + _____

   _____ + _____

4. Down payment on an investment property
that would make sense in today's market   + _____

**Total amount of money that I need to start
my real estate investment program**

$_____ **(A)**

---

*Copyright © 2006 by Walter Sanford. To customize this document, download to your hard drive from www.waltersanford.com/insiderinvestingforms. The document can then be opened, edited, and printed using Microsoft Word or another popular word processing application.

Current Sources of Funds

Available Investment Funds

Liquid/Marketable Assets

Cash (net of required personal safety reserve) $ _____

Savings   _____

Life insurance cash value   _____

Stocks   _____

Bonds   _____

Notes receivable   _____

_____   _____

_____   _____

Subtotal—Liquid/Marketable   + _____

Real Estate Equity Sold and Refinance Proceeds

Value of (nonkeeper) real estate to be sold $ _____

Less: costs of sale   _____

Less: current mortgage balance   _____

Less: taxes   _____

Real Estate Equity   + _____

Available loan amounts on
properties to be held $ _____
                                                    (only refinance to break even)

Less: costs of refinance   _____

Less: current loan balances   _____

Proceeds of Refinancing   + _____

Other Investment Capital

_____   _____

_____   _____

Subtotal—Other Investment Capital   + _____

Total investment funds currently available

$_____ (B)

(continued)

15

Current Sources of Annual Income

Annual Revenues

Annual salary/commission	$ _____
Referral fees	_____
Bonus	_____
Dividends and interest income	_____
Loan payments receivable	_____
Rental Income	_____
Annuities receivable (pension, etc.)	_____

Home-based business (eBay)	_____
Other: _____	_____
Other: _____	_____
Total Revenues	+ _____

Less Expenditures

Office or desk fee	$ _____
Technology acquisition, education, and maintenance	_____
Assistant or temp help	_____
Postage	_____
Printing	_____
Car expense	_____
Office supplies	_____
Personal consumption	_____
Shelter (rent or mortgage payment)	_____
Food	_____
Transportation	_____
Clothing	_____

Energy   _____

Entertainment   _____

Insurance   _____

Repairs and maintenance   _____

Nonreimbursed medical expenses   _____

Charitable and other contributions   _____

Real estate tax on home   _____

Other Schedule C expenses   _____

_____   _____

_____   _____

Subtotal—Personal and Business Consumption   – _____

Less Contractual Obligations

Child support/alimony $_____

Mortgage payments (except residence)   _____

Car loan payments   _____

Installment debt   _____

_____   _____

_____   _____

Subtotal—Contractual Obligations   – _____

Taxes

Federal income taxes   _____

State and city income taxes   _____

Social Security   _____

_____   _____

Total taxes   – _____

Total expenditures   – _____

Amount available for annual investments

$_____(C)

(continued)

So, How Are You Doing?

1. Total needed to start real estate investment program

   – A: _____

2. Assets I can use to pay for "A"

   + B: _____

3. Earnings I can use to pay for "A"

   + C: _____

   + D: _____

Circle positive or negative funds available
for real estate program:

   – D: _____

If your results are positive, congratulations! You may want to increase your
down payment on investment real estate.

If your results are negative, do not worry. You have chosen a business where
you can choose your net income. Continue with the second part of this
planning exercise.

How Much Do I Have to Earn Selling Real Estate?

1. Total amount I am short to start my
   real estate investment program

   – _____ (D)

2. Revenues from last 12 months.

   + _____ (E)

3. Total of lines 1 and 2.

   $_____

4. Multiply line 3 by 140%. Place that dollar amount
   on this line. This will take care of your overhead.

   $_____

5. Divide line 4 by 12 to show monthly earning goals.

   $_____

6. Take 110% of line 5. (This is the total you are
   allowed to spend next year on education.)

   $_____

7. Take 120% of line 6. (This is your total to be
   clear for income taxes.)

   $_____

8. Of my monthly earnings, 80% should come from
   listings sold. (Line 7 x .8)

   $_____

9. Of my monthly earnings, 20% should come from
   sales made. (Line 7 x .20)

   $_____

What I Have to Do to Achieve My Listing and Sales Income

To Achieve My Listing Income:

1. In my market area, the average listing commission is (get this figure from your broker). $_____

2. I must sell the following number of listings per month: (item 8 from previous section divided by preceding item 1).   _____

3. If only 80% of my listings sell, I have to obtain _____ listings per month. (120% of item 2)

4. It may take _____ listing appointments to get a listing (get this number from your broker or sales manager).

5. So, I have to go on _____ listing appointments to get my listings for the month (item 3 x item 4).

6. It may take _____ contacts to get each listing appointment (get this number from your broker or sales manager).

7. So, I have to make _____ contacts each month. (item 5 x item 6).

8. I have to make _____ contacts each week (item 7 divided by item 4).

To Achieve My Sales Income:

1. In my market area, the average sales commission is $_____ (get this number from broker/local board).

2. So, I have to make _____ sales each month to make my goal.

3. It takes about _____ property showings to a qualified buyer to make a sale (get this number from your broker or sales manager).

4. So, I must show _____ properties each month.

5. I must show _____ properties each week.

CHAPTER 4

The Real Estate Agent's Insider Advantages and Fiduciary Responsibilities

Themenu title of this chapter may make some hard-working real estate agents feel uncomfortable, so let me deal with fiduciary duty first.

A real estate agent who takes advantage of clients and commits a breach of trust should be denied a license as a Realtor® and should receive harsh civil and criminal reprimands. That being said, an agent often can achieve a client's goals while performing a real estate transaction that also meets that agent's investment goals. Here are some of the ways that I have accomplished insider transactions in my 30 years of real estate brokerage for my clients:

- One of my systems for monitoring new inventory for my clients is looking at the *hot sheets* every morning. A hot sheet shows all the new listings, sales, withdrawns, and expired listings for that day. When you make hot-sheet viewing a morning habit, you will occasionally come across a property that appears to meet your investment goals. When you pull up more information about the property, you may actually become excited about it. After viewing the property, you find that it is priced correctly and has everything you want.

You write an offer fully describing yourself as a buyer and a licensee, and ask that half of the commission either be paid to your company or be used as a credit to your down payment. This is a legal and ethical transaction. First, you are representing yourself and not the seller by way of your agency disclosures, and second, the seller is agreeing to put the listing out as an offer through the listing agent. Because of your superior knowledge of the area, your ability to add sweat equity through your team, or your judgment that it is an investment that meets your goals, you ethically and morally have the green light to proceed with this transaction.

Be aware that quick flipping of such transactions to another party or excessive and tough negotiations will give you and your company a black eye in the community. Many real estate brokers discourage agents from negotiating on their own behalf to avoid bad feelings between the client or community and the firm. My position is that taking the spoils of your superior knowledge, searching time, and management abilities to quietly find your new investments is the greatest advantage of your license. Nevertheless, this type of purchase seldom happens.

• If I am the listing agent and have disclosed that I would like to purchase the property, I also always disclose that by employing my exclusive marketing, the property might sell for more money than I am offering. In some instances, the sellers have still agreed to sell to me, even after this disclosure. This is a fine line to navigate: As the listing agent, I have a fiduciary duty to provide the best transaction to the seller, but I am buying the property for less than I believe the seller might actually be able to receive. The only way that I can buy a listed property for less than potential market value is by full disclosure. The disclosures must be absolutely brutal. I have put the following disclosure into contracts where I believed I was buying the property for less than market value or less than the listed price:

Seller understands that listing agent has a fiduciary duty to provide the seller with the transaction that meets their goals, explained as the following _____

_____ .

Listing agent has made an offer on the property. Listing agent has stated that this offer may be bettered if marketing is initiated on the property. Seller is free to cancel this transaction at any time prior to closing of this transaction and requests that the property be marketed under the listing agreement. The listing agent/buyer will list and have the property marketed to all potential buyers through all marketing efforts outlined in listing agent's presentation. These marketing efforts include multiple listing service (MLS), signage, networking, and advertising on the Internet and in print. Furthermore, seller understands that if the listing agent closes on this property that the listing agent may later market and sell the property for a profit. Seller further acknowledges that he or she could potentially be selling this property for less than its true value. Sellers are doing this because the listing agent as buyer contemplates completing all aspects of this contract on time, therefore providing surety of close to the seller and meeting all of the other goals mentioned above.

This disclosure should assure anyone that both parties went into the transaction fully informed and that no unfair dealings occurred. This arrangement, however, is a slippery slope and should only be approached with the approval of the full disclosure to a seller by the attorneys for the listing agent and the buyer. (Once the disclosures are made, the seller may not take your offer.)

• While generating leads through avenues such as expireds, for sale by owners, absentee owners, investors, landlords, and mature owners in large homes, you may find sellers who are willing to sell for quick money prior to the execution of a listing agreement. When you find a seller in this situation, as a licensee you should disclose anything that might be unfair to the seller prior to contract.

• Occasionally, you may represent the interest of a buyer who is negotiating a transaction that amazes even you. But in the midst of these negotiations, the buyer becomes a cement head and backs out. You are left with an already negotiated contract, a seller who is willing to proceed on that contract, and no buyer. Many times, I have stepped into my buyer's shoes to complete the transaction. Once again, I use full disclosure if I have the listing. If not, I disclose that I am a licensee.

• It is exciting to me that we get paid for our hard work of generating new buyer and seller leads, then put them together with contracts. While we are providing this service, we can review (for free) the available inventory, listed or unlisted. This opportunity is one of the biggest insider secrets of real estate. We get paid to do a job that allows us to prospect for properties that meet our investment program. The more you do to become a successful real estate agent. By finding buyers and sellers and putting them together, the greater chance you have of finding inventory that meets your investment parameters. Having access to on- and off-market inventory is a valuable insider advantage. You can find sources of off-market inventory in the following ways:

—Meeting sellers who don't list
—Meeting the motivated FSBO (for sale by owner) while looking for inventory for your buyers
—Sending direct mail postcards to owners in an area that a buyer has targeted
—Calling your database of clients and looking for buyers and sellers
—Checking out listings that have not yet hit the MLS but that you have heard about in your office meeting, board meetings, or the "good ole boys" network
—Getting leads about vacant or distressed properties from your lender or from affiliates such as moving companies
—Opportunities that come from your reputation and goodwill

• The nature of the real estate business often puts you in the right place at the right time. You hear a rumor from a lender that something might be coming available; you drive through a neighborhood, see a property in dire need of repair, and a person who turns out to be the owner is standing outside; as you negotiate with a seller, he happens to mention that his next-door neighbor might consider selling. These and other insider tips allow you to be first in line for a potential piece of property either for yourself or for your clients. Just hanging around this business produces gems.

• I have even had instances where the client has begged me to buy the property. My first real estate transaction as an agent, almost 30 years ago now, started with a phone call from a seller in an attractive neighborhood. I made my listing presentation and priced the property correctly. The house sold almost immediately, subject to the sale of the buyer's property. The seller would accept the contract only if I became the listing agent of the second property. That property sold almost immediately, too . . . subject to the sale of a third property. This third property was a little bit out of my area of expertise. Since I was new though, I decided to take on that listing. Although the property made sense as a rental, it remained unsold. When I worked the numbers, I found that selling this third property would allow me to make a 6 percent commission on the first property and a 6 percent commission on the second property. If I purchased the third property, the price could be reduced by my 6 percent commission. The buyers and sellers of transactions one and two begged me to make it happen. Being poor (remember the 1979 debacle described earlier?), I was not in a position to buy, nor did I want to buy, another rental property since I had so many other financial obligations. I went back to all parties involved and asked them to "sweeten the pot"—and they did! In the end, I bought the third property at an approximately 40 percent discount by applying all my commissions and concessions to it. Being a dealmaker as well as a real estate broker is an outstanding insider advantage.

Being an insider in the real estate game is absolutely legal, moral, and ethical, as long as everyone knows what you are doing and you have met your fiduciary duty by disclosing to your clients their property's potential. If you want to add another layer of safety, you can put another real estate agent between yourself and the client you are representing to make certain that the disclosure is as unbiased as possible. Also understand that when two agents work for the same company, even though they represent different parties, this might trigger different agency disclosure requirements. Even though disclosure and agency laws differ from state to state, as long as everyone in the transaction knows everything about the transaction and the agents give the sellers the option to change their mind, it is proper for insiders to find and work the inventory for themselves.

When you use your insider advantage to buy and sell real estate for your own account, having a fiduciary duty to your clients will put you in a challenging position. You need to disclose anything that might affect your clients. As a licensed real estate agent, you have a higher responsibility because of your professional knowledge. You can sum up your responsibility this way: If you do anything that an attorney representing an opposing party could bring up in a court of law as a concern, you need to fully disclose it. It is always wise to go further than necessary to disclose your intentions in real estate dealings, especially when a client is involved, because if you ever do have to spend time in court, I promise you that you will be assumed guilty. You will not be making any money selling real estate because you will spend your time defending an indefensible position created by lack of disclosure in a fiduciary relationship. Here are a few examples of how I protect myself:

- If I am buying a property that I do not have listed, I disclose that I am a real estate agent and my intention is to buy for profit.
- If I am representing a client as a listing agent, I disclose that I am buying for profit, but if we receive a higher offer prior to closing, I will either meet that offer or acquiesce, allowing the seller to sell to the second buyer. I stipulate in detail how much I think that I can make.
- Whenever a client is buying one of my own properties, I further disclose that I am making a profit, and I describe comparable sales in detail so that the buyer knows that this is a fair transaction. Disclosing all challenges with the property is also paramount.

When clients think they are being robbed, agents can go through years of hell that severely affect their lives, future business, current income, and net worth. Likewise, when clients trust their agent, the potential income from future real estate transactions is great.

If I am representing both the buyer and the seller, I make certain that I have in writing—signed, sealed, and delivered—full disclosure of this dual agency position. I clearly inform them of all their options and have them acknowledge that they have chosen me to represent both of them concurrently.

Another smart disclosure is to explain any assignment clauses in your contract. If I buy a property in my name and/or an assignee, I always include the following clause, "The seller acknowledges that the buyer intends to find another buyer and make transfer to that buyer at a higher price and/or better terms. The buyer/agent intends to make a profit in this process."

Overdisclosure not only will save your relationship with a client, but will allow your client to go into the transaction fully informed. Never make a transaction more important than your relationship with the client.

To sum it up, whenever you have an interest as a buyer or a seller, you need to fully disclose that interest and intention. It is only fair to disclose your insider advantage. Honesty is *always* the best policy. People expect you to make a profit on what you do, so disclosing your intentions and potentials does not necessarily affect the transaction.

No single commission or investment return is worth lowering your standards and risking your license. No property is worth risking your ability to make a living. No gain is worth losing a client who not only may repeat buying and selling through you, but also may refer many other clients to you.

Your insider advantage is so strong and so many opportunities present themselves that playing unfair games just does not pay.

CHAPTER 5

Insiders Have the Time to Find High-Quality Investment Properties

S ince you are spending your days earning commission dollars, you have the time to slowly and intelligently contemplate the inventory. You should not be in a hurry here. You are making the same moves as a real estate investor, but you are earning a living while doing it. So, why jump at something that does not make sound business sense? However, once an opportunity presents itself, be able to act quickly. Many agents make poor investment choices because they do not know what a true real estate opportunity looks like. We are using real estate as a vehicle for financial independence that will fund our retirement and provide annuities to our family, communities, and faith. This investment vehicle deserves careful planning.

In the years that I have invested in real estate, I have found that certain situations are nightmares. I know that we have to take some bad with the good, but since we have plenty of time to find superior investments while we are earning money doing it, our insider acquisition plan can be even more stringent than that of your most persnickety investors. As you become more experienced in your real estate brokerage business, you will develop rules that are applicable to your area. Here are some guidelines:

- In most cases, properties located in poor school districts will attract lower paying tenants.
- Generally, older buildings need more expensive repairs than newer buildings.
- One-bedroom units are harder to rent than two-bedroom units. Four-bedroom units can attract multiple family tenants—sometimes in violation of your lease or rental agreements.
- Parking space is always a plus.

- Buy extra land with a building and have the building support that extra land. Land banking is an outstanding method for acquiring land supported by an attached building for future investment.

- Long-term, fixed financing is always safer than short-term or variable financing.

- Properties and buildings in low-income areas usually have higher expense ratios.

- In master-metered buildings, the heat goes on in September and is turned off in May. Furthermore, it can also mean that your apartments look like the LAX landing strip at 11 P.M.

- Outside stairs are expensive.

- Pools cause problems because of maintenance costs and safety requirements.

- Owner-owned washers and dryers in a laundry room are probably not worth the money they make.

- Renting your property with appliances will create as many problems as the property itself.

- If you do not go see where your proposed new tenant currently lives, you deserve what you get.

- The seller's numbers on expenses and income are probably wrong.

- The manager knows the building. If this person wants to continue to manage the property, spending 10 minutes with him or her will be worth days spent with the seller and listing agent.

- Make your inspector/contractor a friend.

- Triple your estimates for repairs to do them correctly.

- A vacancy is better than a bad tenant.

- The city and previous service people will surprise you with their knowledge about a building.

- Another "bus" is always coming by.

This list represents personal investment truths for me. Following these guidelines will help you shortcut or avoid some expensive lessons that I have learned in my life as a real estate agent and real estate investor. Sometimes people have to learn them the hard way. Having a vacant apartment or really wanting to buy a building can lead to mistakes, but these may be mitigated by a lower price or better terms. However, you should never be so eager for a tenant or a building that you overlook the preceding guidelines.

In addition there are six investment rules that I never break:

1. Buy with the intention of never selling.
2. Have no negative cash flow before taxes.
3. Do not use adjustable or variable rate mortgages.
4. Do not allow balloon payments on the underlying mortgages.
5. Do not buy in areas where you have to collect the rent with a gun.
6. Be able to "tire-kick" your investments.

I have learned these rules over the years and have confirmed their value in interviews with successful and financially independent real estate investors. *However, if you apply these rules to satisfying the real estate needs of your clients or investors, your commissioned business will fall off substantially.* There is just not enough inventory that meets these rules. Since you are an insider, you can look at more inventory in less time and get paid while you are doing it. I would expect you to apply a much higher standard to properties you invest in. I never much liked working with investors with high standards—it is just too tough on the buying side.

Here are my reasons for each of these rules:

• *Buy with the intention of never selling.* In general, people who never sell have a higher net worth. Whenever you sell, you have transactional costs and internal revenue costs, sometimes equaling as much as your net profit. If you do not sell, you avoid such costs. In any building or property, there is a learning curve. Once you learn it, you can manage the property more effectively in less time and usually at a lower cost. You also form relationships with the tenants and can negotiate lower costs with supplying vendors. You have time to make changes to minimize the other expenses of the building such as utilities, taxes, and insurance. Owning a building long-term allows you to put its management on autopilot, and also eliminates all the time spent in marketing the building for sale.

Does this mean that I have never sold a building? Absolutely not! I have sold quite a few buildings that I have owned, but only because of mistakes. The buildings were in an area that started to turn bad, a horrific development was constructed next door, or a street-widening ordinance was passed. There are many instances where the dream building that you bought can turn into a nightmare. Some buildings just seem to be cursed. Every tenant you get turns out to be the tenant from hell, and the maintenance never seems to stop. Just as in your real estate business, 20 percent of your clients take up 80 percent of your time. The same is true with your buildings. If you can eliminate the proven losers, your life and the ability to handle other buildings will be enhanced; however, I never go into a purchase with that intention.

So, the general rule still stands—always buy with the intention of never selling. If you do sell, it is not because you *have to* but because you *want to*. When you buy a building that you are never going to sell, you buy it with a different mind-set. It is in a better location, probably with better tenants, long-term better financing, and other considerations that support long-term ownership. Buying with the intention of never selling will make you extremely wealthy in the real estate business, because as one of my friends always says, "Equity happens!" On autopilot are price, rent appreciation, amortization, tax benefits, and the equity developed from improvements. Leverage accentuates all these factors. Don't mess it up by selling.

   • *Have no negative cash flow before taxes.* This is one of the hardest rules to keep, because cash flow presents so many questions. First, let me clear up one of the most common mistakes in real estate—cash flow before or after tax benefits. If cash flow is created after you factor in the income tax benefits of owning a building, it is a fleeting benefit.

   Tax laws change; furthermore, your income situation can change, which can affect your tax situation. Since buyers come in many tax brackets, who is to say that your buyer needs those same tax benefits if you sell the building? Never let the tax tail wag the investment dog: Tax benefits are "gravy." The building must stand on its own as an investment vehicle. The minimum investment return that I will accept on a building is that the property breaks even, meaning its income pays all expenses. I make one small concession in that I will add equity paydown on the loan back into cash flow. This creates a real cash flow negative, but since the equity paydown is actually a bank account that is growing, I will add that back into my cash flow.

   What about appreciation? This is an outstanding concept, but many times in the past 30 years, there has been *depreciation* instead of appreciation. If you buy a building based on appreciation and there is none, you may have to sell the building, which will mean breaking rule 1.

   If you are an insider, you can spend the time to find a building that makes sense without having to factor in a nebulous market direction that may or may not materialize. It is plain and simple. You can buy real estate that breaks even after considering the equity paydown. You have the time to do it—you just need to know *how* to do it.

   Ownership of a piece of real estate involves many expenses: management, property taxes, insurance, repair or replacement of major systems, vacancy factor, maintenance factor, utilities, landscaping, tenant turnaround costs, legal fees, accounting fees, advertising, and every other Schedule E expense you can think of. The problem with this is that you will seldom get true figures from a seller; furthermore, since you have so much property to evaluate, you do not have the time to make exhaustive discovery expeditions on every building. In fact, good ones may be so desirable that if you want them, you are going to have to evaluate them quickly. Although you can buy properties with exploratory contingencies, it is best to know as much as you can about your go/no-go plan as soon as possible. The only way to do this is by applying an expense factor to the building. A lender will typically use 25 percent of rents as the expense factor for buildings with five or more apartments. I have never owned a building that had only a 25 percent expense factor when I included a vacancy factor in the worst of rental markets and repair and replacement factors for heating and air conditioning units, water heaters, roofs, and other major expenses. If your building cannot breakeven sans equity paydown with a 40 percent expense factor, I would go back and sharpen my pencil or find another building. That means 40 percent of market rents will eventually go to pay all your expenses, except for income taxes. When you use this 40 percent expense factor, you have 60 percent left to fully amortize your loan, except for equity paydown, as discussed earlier. To guarantee that you have a break even or positive cash flow property, use a quick 40 percent expense ratio factor to let you know how much you can pay for a building while earmarking 60 percent of its market rents to take care of the debt service. No negative cash flow means no pain, which means no rush to sell in a bad market. Once you know how large a loan 60 percent of market income will amortize, you can divide that amount by 90 percent to come up with a potential purchase price with 10 percent down.

• *Do not use adjustable or variable rate mortgages.* As this book is being written, a lot of "cheap" money is available. That has not always been the case. Many lenders do not like to give long-term fixed loans to five or more units; in fact, there are many investment properties where no fixed money is available. You will have to consider that as an additional risk factor, if needed. Have I taken additional risk factors on properties? Of course. When you recognize adjustable or variable rate mortgages as a risk factor, you will want concessions in other areas of negotiation on the building. When you obtain a variable interest rate mortgage at the top of the market, it probably can only get better. When you obtain a variable interest rate mortgage at the bottom of the market, it can probably only get worse. When variable interest rates go up, higher mortgage payments will be the result. If rents do not keep up (which they normally do not), you will create a negative cash flow position—violating rule 2. Then, if you cannot handle a negative cash flow position, you will be forced to violate rule 1.

Having a known quantity concerning your interest outgo, once again allows you to put this building on autopilot. It also determines a standard at which you will run the building to achieve the rents necessary to amortize this loan. Knowing the future is all important. Since I have seen interest rates range all the way from 4.7 percent to 23 percent—I am gun-shy about allowing a financial institution to have control of my future. Fixed, fully amortized loans provide peace.

• *Do not put balloon payments on the underlying mortgages.* Along the same theme, a short-term balloon payment provides an unknown factor in your investment future. When that short-term balloon payment is due in 3, 5, or 10 years, will you have enough money to pay it? Will mortgage rates be affordable to refinance it? Will secondary money be available? Adding unknowns to your real estate investment future will cause you to rethink the initial transaction. If long-term, fully amortized money is not available, I am going to have to ask, "Why not?" Some of you will say that you are always at the mercy of a lending institution. Let me correct you. Some of my favorite transactions have occurred with the sellers carrying back the financing. If you cannot tell me what the future will be when your loan comes due, then I have to consider that as a negative factor in your purchase decision. I have some alternatives to institutional financing for you.

• *Do not buy in areas where you have to collect the rent with a gun.* I say this tongue in cheek; in fact, I have been taken to task a few times. The question is, "What about people who need housing? How about supplying a service to the less fortunate?" These are extremely worthy goals, but not in the context of this book— successful real estate systems for an insider investor. You have the time to find the best real estate. Buying properties in a less desirable area may provide housing for needy people, but is unlikely to have the highest return. You say, "The income-to-price ratio is so much better, Walter!" What you are saying is that you are receiving a higher income for the same-price building. This might be true, but once you figure in the hassle and higher expense factors, you might also be wrong. Some of these areas engender less pride in ownership, and tenants take less care in maintaining their home. In the end, it is the owner's responsibility to repair any deferred maintenance, and this equates to higher expenses. Turnover also is higher because people in low socioeconomic groups have less certain cash flows. If you want to provide a service to the less fortunate, then I am 100 percent behind you; however, you cannot pretend it is your best investment alternative. Appreciation will also be lower.

• *Be able to tire-kick your investments.* You may believe that properties meeting the preceding criteria are not available in your area. Except for some parts of the bay area in California, I am not aware of any place within a two-hour drive where you cannot buy properties that come close to meeting these parameters. The reality of investing in distant real estate is simply this—when you invest in properties far from your home and cannot make many unannounced inspections, you will pay large sums to hire either an on-site or off-site manager. You cannot have a building cash flow where maintenance workers are charging you $45 to change a light bulb. Having control through "drive-bys" has always allowed me to nip tenancy problems in the bud and to discover preventive maintenance items. It is amazing how much more concerned the eyes of an owner are compared with those of a manager. Even though you say the numbers are better in other states, I promise you that the difference in caring, concerned, and alert management by owners versus hired managers will mitigate those differences. When you are an insider, you have a pretty good handle on the business in your local area. You know about the new

Wal-Mart coming in, the new defense contracts pending, or the fact that business will be moving out of your state next year. You can take the temperatures of buyers and sellers. You can formulate plans for further acquisition or the cutting of losses. When you invest in another state, you give up these insider advantages. You do not have a feeling for the local business area or real estate climate. The closer to home that you can make your investments, the more control you will have in implementing your investment plan. Your real estate business is in town. Your investments should be close by, too.

Thus far in this chapter, we have discussed my mandatory plan. From time to time in this system, I voice some concerns and raise red flags that you should watch out for. These are not rules, but can help you find a building that you can live with long enough to allow the tenants to pay off your mortgage. *This concept is where I run into difficulty with insiders of different investment philosophies.*

You are either an investor or a speculator. If you are a speculator, you are depending on the building to go up in value, and you place less credence on the operation of that building as a business. If you are an investor, the building must operate as a business and amortize the debt. The problem with being a speculator is that you do not control the direction of the appreciation of real estate. Real estate in Southern California dropped 15 percent to 30 percent in the early 1980s. In the early 1990s, real estate dropped 30 percent to 40 percent. Based on the current bubble theories and the run-up in real estate in 2006, there is a high probability that this drop could happen again in our greatly inflated real estate price areas.

People who buy a long-term asset (real estate) with short-term thoughts (violations of rules 1 through 6) might find that when appreciation stagnates or becomes depreciation, buying properties based on speculation will quickly lose its charm. I have never gone wrong buying buildings that make sense as businesses; in fact, they have appreciated as well as or better than buildings bought for speculation. Furthermore, they could weather all storms. The real estate speculator who has gone through a storm will long someday to be called *a real estate investor.*

When I was young, my goal was to own 400 free-and-clear units. I have reduced that goal to a lesser amount because of mistakes that I have made in my life; however, the substantial real estate portfolio that I acquire under my rules for success will be owned by me—free and clear. The complaint that I hear about this plan is, "Where does the investment money come from?" That is why it is so important to be an insider. When you are a successful real estate broker and are using my systems or have other mentors with systems that work, you will find that you will make enough money in commissions to fund your down payments and your other dreams. I had to have an overriding reason for working hard as a real estate agent to make net proceeds in commissions. My reason was to buy the product that I sold, touched, felt, and evaluated every day.

When you buy this product correctly with proceeds from your net cash flow of commissions and manage it using the same systems you are using to manage your business, your tenants will pay that property off and someday allow you to say—"I love this business of real estate brokerage, but I don't have to go to work today!"

Someday, your rental income may replace your commission income. It will allow you to live the life that you have always dreamed about. You might like to see this happen a little faster than nine years, which is the current average amortization of my loans, based on all my cash flow being applied to the payment. Since you are making money implementing the successful real estate systems described in this book, you can apply the positive cash flow from your real estate commission business toward your underlying investment property loans. This will help you amortize them quickly. It is the *snowball theory* of my real estate investment program.

By making principal paydowns funded by the positive cash flow on an intelligently purchased property, you accelerate the amortization schedule to the point where the property becomes free and clear and positive cash flow is the order of the day. The day when you get your first building free and clear is an indescribably magnificent occasion.

You now have a decision to make: To which of your current buildings should you apply all the positive cash flow? The answer is the one that will create the most positive cash flow the fastest or the one that has the mortgage with the highest interest rate. Since you are still working hard in the real estate brokerage business and earning a great living, you move the positive cash flow from your first free and clear building to the next one. The next building snowballs even faster with the additional positive cash flow from your other buildings. The second building will be paid off faster, thus facilitating the third, fourth, fifth, and so on.

This is the third time that I have made a fortune in real estate investing. The first time, you already have read about. My not having a life caused me to lose most of my second round of smart real estate investments through divorce. This system, if not my life, has been foolproof for me and it will be for you also. I intend to run my life successfully so that I do not have to build a portfolio a fourth time.

Many of my coaching clients have reached financial independence in a short time using this system. Being an insider allows you to take your time to find the buildings that create positive cash flow, allows you to apply the positive cash flow to the underlying loans, and lets you use real estate brokerage to fund your life and down payments. This puts you in a position to slowly and intelligently find properties that meet your insider parameters and that allow the snowball theory to work.

CHAPTER 6

Combining Investing with Seller Lead Generation in Your Brokerage Business

The first rule in a real estate brokerage business is to *get listings*. It may help you to follow this rule if you understand that you can control listings better than you can control buyers. It is faster and less expensive to obtain a commission from a listing than from a buyer because buyers take more personal hand-holding than listings do. Obtaining a listing is the least expensive and most effective way to find a buyer. Promoting listings geographically by signs, word of mouth, and worldwide through the Internet will put you in front of more buyers with less work.

When I start coaching new real estate agents, I immediately build their brokerage business cash flow by implementing new seller lead generation systems. The majority of the world's top agents spend much of their time planning, implementing, and monitoring their seller lead generation programs. The most successful real estate agents in the country time-block their schedules to make certain that nothing interferes with their seller lead generation systems. It is simple—the top agents list and make a lot of money doing it.

Since you are paid to list and sell properties, you have discovered how wonderful it is to be a real estate agent and investor at the same time. You get paid to prospect for investment inventory. As you are generating leads to find sellers, you are also viewing those pieces of inventory. As you meet those sellers, you can evaluate whether their properties fit your investment profile. If they do not (which is usually the case), you still get paid to list and sell the property. On the off chance that the property meets your parameters, you have the opportunity to develop a win/win situation. Many times, win/win situations have given me my most satisfying real estate experiences.

In generating leads from hot seller demographics—expireds, for sale by owners, long-time owners, absentee owners, multiple property owners, and mature owners in large properties—I have found many people who needed a quick sale. Real estate is a fairly nonliquid investment. Achieving liquidity requires an evaluation of the property, a marketing program, and a sales period. If you, as a real estate agent, can be the buyer, it eliminates the marketing period You can also accelerate the sales period because of your connections with your team members, such as escrow, title, and mortgage companies. You can close this property faster and more effectively than an outside buyer; you have already evaluated it when you prepared the listing presentation. This sometimes is a real asset to a seller. Someone who has a compelling reason to immediately become liquid might be a good prospect if the property meets your investment criteria. People have many reasons for selling quickly. Here are some that I have encountered:

* *A life-changing event.* I have had sellers who needed to relocate immediately, usually because one of the "D" words—death, divorce, disillusion, and debt. The "D" words have been a staple for higher real estate agent incomes for many years. Many things can happen in a person's life to necessitate a quick sale. A real estate agent who is equipped as a real estate investor can sometimes be the fastest to the closing table. If the agent fully discloses the value of the property and provides a win/win situation for all parties involved, it is one of the advantages of selling real estate and being an investor at the same time.

* *Burnout.* Often, a seller is tired of dealing with tenants or management companies. I have seen sellers who have been driven to bankruptcy by really bad tenants. Sometimes there is a limit to the amount of abuse that a seller can receive from a tenant or a management company; however, the proper management of real estate is a systemized process. When something does not work correctly, it is usually because the owner does not know the golden rules of management. People who are burned out in real estate investments have created a large part of my inventory. Many of these sellers were willing to negotiate with me for the purchase of their property rather than spend one more moment trying to collect rents.

* *Another deal.* This is an outstanding method of not only helping the seller but also increasing your investment inventory. I have met many sellers who needed the proceeds to purchase another property. Sometimes they had found a better deal. Or they might have been involved in an exchange and that transaction fell through. Sometimes they wanted to increase their depreciation write-off or cash flow. Whatever the reason, the new transaction would not wait, and they had to become liquid on their current ownership. Once again, being an insider with the know-how to be an investor offers advantages to both parties.

* *IRC (Internal Revenue Code) tax deferred exchange.* You might be dealing with an investor who is in the middle of a Section 1031 tax deferred exchange and must adhere to strict time considerations. This happens when the investor is selling multiple properties and trying to obtain a new one. Since the current laws in tax de-

ferred exchanges say that the taxpayer must identify the new property within 45 days of the sale of the old property and close within 6 months of the sale of the old property, strict time considerations necessitate selling the downleg properties. If I have sold some of the downleg properties for the person involved with the exchange and other properties remain to be sold to complete the exchange, the investor can see the wisdom in selling one of unsold properties to me to complete the exchange.

• *The "Informal Domino" theory.* This situation, as discussed earlier, starts with a house being sold subject to the sale of another house. If that property is then sold subject to another property being sold, and on down the line, it soon becomes necessary for the last property to be sold before all the other dominos can fall. When there is no buyer for the last listed property, you can sometimes get numerous stipends from commissions and motivated clients by buying that first domino (if it meets your investment parameters).

• *Financial conditions.* A seller may have to raise a lot of cash for personal reasons—the quicker, the better. Once again, the real estate agent with the ability to be an investor is in the right place at the right time, helping the seller receive the necessary funds. I have even helped "innocent until proven guilty" clients who needed to sell their property to obtain funds for their legal defense.

• *Retirement.* The sellers may decide to sell their properties and ride off into the sunset. If they are willing to take a tax hit of a sale without an exchange, the lure of marlin fishing off Cabo may necessitate a fast and efficient sale that I can certainly offer.

These situations and more occur as you work day in and day out obtaining listing leads. It is one of the perks of being an insider investor. You will find that being in this business introduces you to potential sellers whom you would have never otherwise met. Talking with people at open houses and going on a listing presentation where you discover that the seller owns other property are all potential sources of investment property. It is important to stay alert for opportunities to find a property that meets your investment needs. Every property you meet in the course of your real estate brokerage business could be your next investment.

CHAPTER 7

Brokers and Agents: Buyers Are Bad; Insiders: Buyers Are Good

From the standpoint of a real estate brokerage, handling buyers is an expensive and time-consuming activity, but from an insider investor's standpoint, buyers can be lucrative.

A top real estate agent who handles buyers in today's market qualifies them in several ways. The agent first asks a series of questions to determine their level of motivation. Second, a known lender must preapprove the buyers for a mortgage on the property being considered. Third, the buyers must meet with the real estate agent in person to discuss a possible agreement. Finally, at the end of the conference, the buyers are required to sign a loyalty or buyer brokerage agreement that cements the relationship between them and the agent. The buyers agree to buy a piece of property exclusively from that agent, and if they then buy a property from someone else (no matter what entity), they will still owe the first and contracted agent a full commission.

Top agents get buyers to sign such an agreement by offering amazing services that no one else can match. These services include showing the buyer unique, special, and even secret properties at better than retail prices. Agents find these unusual properties by following inventory leads from several sources, such as their past-client database (people who own a piece of real estate like the one the buyers are seeking). Agents then contact these people to see if they might be interested in selling. They also look at all expired listings whose parameters meet those of the buyers. These unsuccessful sellers are contacted to determine their interest level in selling. Most top real estate agents have a good relationship with a majority of the for-sale-by-owner sellers in the area and can discuss with them the terms of sale, which would include a commission. Remember, the buyers have signed an agreement, so even if they decide to buy the for-sale-by-owner property and no commission is available, the agreement could commit the buyers to pay the real estate commission.

The next source of inventory comes from a direct mailing to the buyers' area of interest. The mailing announces that the agent has buyers who are prequalified and who are looking for properties meeting certain parameters in that neighborhood. The mailing asks any interested sellers to contact the agent. Inventory also may come from lender affiliates who might know of distressed, foreclosure, or pre-foreclosure properties that the bank might either own or expect to own soon.

These sources of unique leads are in addition to contributions from the rumor mill, where agents can hear of inventory that has not quite hit the market. The ability to provide all this inventory to buyers provides the impetus to their signing a loyalty or buyer brokerage agreement. The same incentive that encourages the buyer to sign the agreement forces the agent to search out the inventory. The pure act of obtaining inventory that is not readily available through the multiple listing service positions the agent as the first person to meet the seller's needs. Once more, the agent is being paid to find pieces of inventory that meet personal investment goals.

Buyers have also been some of my greatest teachers. Having buyers as mentors is a major attribute of being an insider investor in the real estate business. Many times, I have observed buyers buy properties that I thought could not produce a return. I did not understand where the value came from.

I remember a client who bought a triplex in Long Beach, California. His keen eye had allowed him to determine that two of the units could be reconfigured and made into three, therefore increasing the income of the property inexpensively. It was done with permits, and there was enough parking for the city to give its blessing. He immediately increased the value of the property by $125,000 with only a $30,000 capital improvement. The blueprint provided by this buyer helped me to find triplexes of similar configuration and do the same thing.

Another client bought a duplex on a multifamily/higher-density lot. The buyer, who bought the property without disclosing his intentions, made me scratch my head as I tried to imagine how there would ever be a profit. Six months later, he listed the new fourplex with me, and then I totally understood his "insane" purchase. He had bought the duplex and then put in another duplex at the back of the property. He did all this with the blessings of the city and more than doubled the property's value for less than 30 percent of the cost of the original duplex.

One of my buyers, later turned friend, developed a unique idea of buying vacant land near major hospitals and offering professional condominiums for doctors, accountants, and attorneys. The concept has been so hot that he still sells out some elevations and floor plans before workers put a shovel into the ground.

The buyer as mentor is a great learning device for agents who want to become successful investors. By representing buyers who have considerable knowledge of investments, agents soon learn to invest as they do—profitably and intelligently.

Another insider task that is extremely valuable is the negotiation of contracts. As you meet buyers or your sellers become buyers, you get automatic practice in writing successful contracts. This is where I learned what I can accomplish for my clients with contract clauses that add profit to the transaction. These techniques are discussed in other chapters, but many of the contract clauses that I have developed for my buyers I have incorporated into my personal investing practice to better achieve my goals. Every new real estate agent uses experiences with clients to become a more successful professional. As an insider, you should look at every buyer as an opportunity to practice writing offers for properties that you will one day purchase yourself.

As an offshoot of the preceding lesson, it has been extremely profitable for me to negotiate transactions where my buyers leave off. Many times, mutual offers and counteroffers are passed back and forth. Sometimes to my dismay, the buyer drops out of negotiations because of frustration or exhaustion. On occasion, after my buyers have dropped out of negotiations, I have stepped in to take the buyers' place (with their blessings). A buyer may work with a piece of property as if it were a lump of clay, shape it into something great, pass on the whole situation, and hand it over to me. Being at the right place at the right time is accentuated and accelerated when you are the insider broker between a unmotivated buyer and a motivated seller.

Another advantage of being an insider is to take advantage of the relationships that you have built by meeting sellers through buyers. Frequently, I have successfully completed transactions for my buyers, thus meeting the sellers. These sellers have gone on to do business with me—sometimes under the brokerage banner and sometimes as the providers of inventory for my personal investment account.

Your goal is to build a referral business, where successful clients send you additional leads because you treat everyone fairly, morally, and ethically. Some of these are sellers who provide you with the inventory necessary to complete transactions for your personal investment goals. The bottom line is that you are getting paid as a real estate broker while you search out the option of being an insider investor. Many times, the value of being an insider is learning terms that are more important than price.

CHAPTER 8

Insider Terms

I always say, "I'll pay you anything you want, as long as I get the right terms." Terms are often much more important than price. By using your insider advantages in your counseling with sellers as well as being a participant in the negotiations with your buyers, you can often find terms that fit your investment portfolio so well that you become the person most willing to pay for the property.

Sometimes, you may need alternatives to institutional lending because of a poor FICO (credit) score or because of exceeding Fannie Mae and Freddie Mac guidelines for the number of nonowner-occupied investor loans allowed at fixed rates. Currently, that rule is maxed out at 10 properties or loans. After you have received 10 nonowner-occupied investor loans, whether houses or apartment buildings, the secondary market will not allow institutional lenders to give you any more fixed money, which places you in the variable/adjustable rates mortgages and violates one of our rules. Whether the market turns and money dries up or you will soon exceed your 10-loan maximum—someday you will be looking for alternatives to institutional financing.

One of the best possibilities is seller financing. There are many reasons sellers might want to finance their own property:

• The sellers have a large amount of cash and are looking for an investment vehicle. When you offer a 5, 6, 7, or 8 percent return on the current market, they are motivated to accept it, especially when the loan is secured by an asset that they know and trust—their building.

• Often, sellers do not qualify for any tax advantages on a sale and will owe capital gains on the full profit unless the transaction is an installment sale. In an installment sale, the sellers carry back a large portion of the proceeds as the mortgage. They actually loan you the money to buy their property. This loan is represented by a first mortgage or trust deed on the property. The payments are stated by an attached promissory or mortgage note. The Internal Revenue Service (IRS) says that these seller-carryback or seller-financed loans are installment sales.

This means that the sellers only need to pay capital gains taxes on the profit as they receive it. The sellers' taxes are spread over the time period for the mortgage note. Because of this benefit, the sellers are earning interest on money that they would otherwise owe to the IRS. This substantially increases the return on the sellers' carryback and motivates them to provide this opportunity to you.

• The sellers have relatives who are inheriting the proceeds of the sale. These relatives might not be able to accept large sums of cash because of their immaturity or inability to manage money. The sellers may find that a promissory note is the perfect solution to provide a long-term annuity to these relatives.

• Real estate sales often happen during an unsympathetic market. Anything and everything has to be done to improve the value of the property. One of the options is to offer preferential terms.

• Sellers also may carry back financing from a speculator's standpoint. If there is a default on the note, they can keep the down payment, then foreclose on the mortgage or trust deed, and regain ownership of the property. This can only come into play if the down payment was sufficient enough to compensate the owners for the time and costs of foreclosure plus any damage done to the property while under the buyer's ownership.

There are many reasons for a seller to accept a seller carryback, but there are also strong reasons for a buyer to negotiate a seller carryback:

• The interest rate may be preferential over institutional terms, and there are usually no costs in the acquisition of the loan.

• Usually, a credit report or FICO score is less important to sellers than it is to a bank because sellers do not have to report to shareholders on the secondary market. It is still important for the sellers to obtain financial background documents on the buyer, so that if they ever wanted to sell their note, they would have proof that the payer on the note is financially viable.

• Another advantage of seller carryback financing is that these loans can be fully amortized with no balloon payments and no due-on-sale clauses. In fact, the promissory note can be written in almost any manner for both the buyer and seller engaged in a win-win transaction.

• Another advantage of a seller carryback note is that the owner of the property with a seller carryback note as a lien on the property might be able to sell the property. This would allow the new buyer to assume the original terms of that note. Furthermore, the seller who bought the property from the original seller who carried back the note might be able to sell the property and wrap the existing financing at a higher interest rate. This means that the first buyers, who obtained the seller carryback financing, not only would receive a return of interest on any equity carried back, but also would receive an override above the amount of interest that they paid out on the underlying loan, as long as a higher rate was charged on the wrap than what was on the underlying loans.

• Another advantage in a horrific real estate market is that a buyer can ask the original seller of the property to accept the property back without filing for foreclosure. In this transaction, called a *deed in lieu of foreclosure,* the buyer returns the property to the original seller. The reason they might be interested in doing this is that the sellers do not have to start a foreclosure, there are no costs, and there is no downtime on a building that may be under poor management. The advantage for the buyers is that no foreclosure or credit problems would be reported on their account. In a really bad market, the sellers might even be willing to renegotiate the note in order not to get the property back.

There are numerous ways to finance a property when the seller is willing to "be the bank." Negotiating the terms of a note is just as important as negotiating the sale of the real estate. All concepts of fiduciary duty and disclosure are paramount in these negotiations. If you are a real estate agent negotiating a note and trust deed for yourself and it is not in the client's best interest, this is just as serious a violation of your fiduciary duty as stealing a piece of property at a below-market price. Items like late charges, due on sale clauses, and other terms make the loan safer for the original owners; sellers need to understand whether they are included in the note.

Another huge advantage of seller carryback financing for a buyer is that the payout can be negotiated to meet the start-up needs of the new buyer. If the buyer has purchased a property that needs substantial refurbishment to bring it up to market rents, then possibly a seller carryback mortgage or trust deed could be written specifying no payments, interest only, or less than fully amortized payments to give the buyer an additional source of funds for necessary repairs. Sellers might be willing to do this because all improvements make their security worth more money.

As you are meeting sellers and negotiating for buyers, you will soon learn how to determine a seller's needs. When you establish that a seller carryback mortgage would meet a seller's needs better than cash and those same terms help the buyer (possibly yourself), you will be in a position to negotiate agreeable terms because of your insider status; and the end result will also be a win for the seller.

The better the terms, the faster you will obtain a free-and-clear property, thus meeting the goals of this book and system. This is a huge tool in your insider tool kit to help you maximize net income on your real estate investment.

CHAPTER 9

Insider Net Income Analysis

The first step in looking at a property is to determine the income it will likely produce. Income determines everything. Since I follow a long-term hold strategy, the properties need to break even or have positive cash flow eventually! It is important that you determine income and expenses before you get too far into the purchase of a building. Be aware, however, that overanalysis can kill. I have had many clients who suffered from *paralysis of analysis*. Many transactions are lost by not saying "Yes" with dispatch.

Become adroit in working the numbers quickly. Determining income is more an art than an accounting problem. You want to look at two types of income: existing and potential. Existing income is what the current owner, whether efficient or not, is bringing in from the investment. Potential income is what happens after applying genius management and making talented changes. One of the most important skills that an investor can possess is the ability to examine a building and accurately forecast its operating income.

As an insider, you should use a checklist because your familiarity with buildings may cause you to forget important aspects. Sellers and their real estate agents generally provide prospective purchasers with projected operating statements as part of their marketing effort. Being an insider, you know you must ignore these statements. The forms almost always include exaggerated income figures and underrealized expenses. No matter how much confidence you have in the owner or the cooperative real estate agent, the operating statement is too important for you to rely on anything but your own insider eye. It is virtually impossible for anyone but you to predict your operating expenses, because some of them will vary according to the way you manage. You might want 100 percent occupancy, but others might accept vacancies to get top-dollar rents.

Constructing an accurate operating statement is a three-step process. First, you must identify all the incoming expense items that apply to the property. Next, you must verify the items that can be verified. Finally, you must estimate the things that vary according to the way you manage the property.

Rent is not the only type of income (see Form 9.1). Any of the other items listed on the form are or could be produced by the building. Also, be alert to income not listed on this form.

The next step is to determine the expenses on the property. Form 9.2 is my checklist of the expenses that I have had on my properties. You can use this list to make certain that you are taking all expense areas into account.

Substantial research is necessary to determine the income and expenses involved with a property. As an insider, I made most of my purchases quickly and verified my numbers after I had tied up the property. Make your offer subject to your verification of income and expenses, prior to having all your ducks in a row. I have been very successful in determining what repairs will be needed for a property to bring in market income. Your insider insights should help you increase your income based on your experiences negotiating contracts for your buyers and sellers.

As far as expenses are concerned, I have consistently used a 40 percent expense factor in my 30 years of investing. As mentioned earlier, this is a 15 percent increase over the calculations banks use on income-producing property, but my figure is correct. When you look at all the expenses listed in Form 9.2, you will find that many of them equal 35 to 40 percent—even more than 40 percent in tough areas. If you need to make a decision quickly, 40 percent of potential income is a safe estimate.

Don't let *paralysis of analysis* lose a great transaction for you. One of the greatest gifts that you receive as an insider is your introduction to property that other people have not yet heard about, but you may have to move fast and confidently. It is to your advantage to use your experience to make fast decisions. After you have negotiated the contract, you can go back and dot your i's and cross your t's by going through Form 9.2 in detail. You have lots of time to see all the opportunities your insider status affords you but get ready to pull the trigger when one hits the bull's-eye.

Downloadable FORM 9.1
Income from Building*

Garage rent:	$_____
Laundry income:	$_____
Swim club income:	$_____
Rent on stores or offices:	$_____
Signage:	$_____
Oil royalties:	$_____
Parking:	$_____
Easements:	$_____
Cellular towers:	$_____
Security and pet deposits:	$_____
Rent increases coming from repairs or construction changes:	$_____

*Copyright © 2006 by Walter Sanford. To customize this document, download to your hard drive from www.waltersanford .com/insiderinvestingforms. The document can then be opened, edited, and printed using Microsoft Word or another popular word processing application.

Downloadable FORM 9.2
Expenses for Property*

Fees

Alarm permit: _____

Health permit: _____

Accountant's fees: _____

Attorney's fees: _____

Government inspection fees: _____

Property management fees: _____

Business license: _____

Rent control board: _____

Parking fees: _____

Land lease: _____

Insurance

Boiler insurance: _____

Fidelity bond insurance: _____

Fire and casualty insurance: _____

Flood insurance: _____

Liability insurance: _____

Pool insurance: _____

Worker's compensation: _____

Umbrella policy: _____

Maintenance

Air conditioning services: _____

Cleaning apartments: _____

Blinds/drapes cleaning: _____

Elevator services: _____

Extermination: _____

Heating system service: _____

Landscaping: _____

Painting: _____

Pool service: _____

Repairs: _____

Carpet cleaning: _____

Snow removal: _____

Graffiti: _____

Pest or termite control: _____

*Copyright © 2006 by Walter Sanford. To customize this document, download to your hard drive from www.waltersanford .com/insiderinvestingforms. The document can then be opened, edited, and printed using Microsoft Word or another popular word processing application.

(continued)

Payroll

FICA (Social Security Tax): _____

FUTA (Federal Unemployment Tax):_____

Leasing agent payroll:_____

Maintenance payroll:_____

State disability tax: _____

State unemployment tax: _____

Manager: _____

Property Taxes

Include personal property taxes: _____

Replacement Reserves

Appliance replacement: _____

Carpet replacement:_____

Common area interior painting:_____

Exterior painting:_____

Furniture replacement:_____

Pool resurfacing:_____

Tuck-pointing brickwork: _____

Roof replacement: _____

Water heater: _____

Mailboxes: _____

Gates/security: _____

Heating/air conditioning:_____

Utilities

Electricity: _____

Gas/oil: _____

Rubbish removal: _____

Sewer:_____

Telephone: _____

Water: _____

Cable/Internet: _____

Vacancy Factor

Your vacancy rate will be a function of the rent you charge and the overall quality of management and the building. If the present owner is enjoying a consistent 100 percent occupancy rate and you plan to charge similar rents, there is no point in adding a 5 percent vacancy rate into your calculations. On the other hand, if you plan to raise rents substantially, you should probably include a large vacancy estimate. You can verify the present owner's vacancy rate by checking the dates on his leases: _____

Miscellaneous

A. Advertising (newspaper, signs, rental agency, Internet): _____

   _____

B. When the building is not located on a high traffic street, owners often obtain permission from the owner of a property on a strategic corner to pitch a sign that will direct prospective tenants to the property. These signs can be extremely important to your marketing effort, and the monthly rental fee paid to the landowner is an unavoidable expense that can be easily overlooked:_____

C. Apartment Owners Association dues:_____. Some associations assess their members a flat dollar amount for each apartment. Be sure to include this incremental cost in your annual expense.

D. Credit Reports: _____

E. Security Deposit Interest: _____

   Many states require that all or part of this interest be paid to tenants.

F. Homeowner's assessments: _____

Verification

Some expenses can be verified by speaking with the appropriate supplier or government agency. Don't hesitate to do so. Call the municipal government and ask about the following:

What is the total property assessment? _____

Assessment for land? _____

Improvements? _____

Will the property be reassessed upon sale? _____

If not, when is the next reassessment scheduled? _____

What is the current tax rate? _____

Any indications of next year's rate? _____

Are any municipal improvements pending? _____

Is the municipal government considering rent control legislation? _____

Water: _____

Sewage:_____

Electricity:_____

Trash Removal:_____

Speak with the municipal water and sewage departments and other utilities (electricity, trash removal, and so forth), and ask if they will give you figures for your prospective property for the past three years. Request any available information about future rate increases._____

Call all service vendors from the last year and ask if all recommended service was carried out._____

Other: _____

   _____

   _____

CHAPTER 10

Your Real Estate Insider Team

One of the most exciting assets of being a real estate agent insider is that you already have a great team of advisors to help your clients. These advisors make a living off your listings and sales and therefore treat you not only as a valuable client but also as a source of future business. These service providers, commonly called *affiliates* in the real estate industry, pull out all the stops when servicing their real estate agent/broker clients.

Affiliates liked my brokerage because we were very loyal to their services. Once I found affiliates who took extremely good care of my clients, I tried to include them in every transaction. On receiving a real estate offer, I would counteroffer the cooperating real estate agent to include many of my affiliate service givers. Most top real estate agents control the inventory listing side of the business. During my listing presentation, I was adept at convincing the seller that I could not guarantee the quality or outcome of the transaction without my team of professionals. My sellers understood that having a team that was loyal to me increased their chances of meeting their goals.

When an offer came in from a cooperative real estate agent, it was easy for me to counteroffer the use of my affiliates. These affiliates appreciated the effort, consistently held me in high esteem, and jumped a little higher for me. My affiliates felt free to call and solicit other real estate agents, knowing that their account with me was secure.

I assembled the counteroffer in a nonthreatening manner to prevent losing the transaction. If a cooperative agent brought in another lender to handle the transaction for their buyers, my counteroffer would say that the buyers had to be preapproved through my lender. But I would add that after preapproval, the buyers were free to use any lender of their choice. This gave my lender a chance to meet with the buyers before they submitted a loan application. If my lender showed up with a businesslike manner and presented outstanding opportunities to achieve the buyers' goals, they were likely to accept the invitation for financing after the application process. My lender received a substantial income from the loans I directed through this system. Countering the lender's name in the contract garnered much more business; it cemented our relationship and guaranteed that my lender provided me with every advantage whenever the loan was for me.

My lender and I also explored opportunities of joint lead generation in financing for-sale-by-owner properties. Working as the first contact, this lender would also approach divorcing couples to refinance their property prior to the spousal transfer. Not only did these systems help my business, they also filled my lender's pipeline. As mentioned, a side benefit of this partnership was that, when I had my own needs, I received every kindness and consideration.

It is important for insiders to use affiliates, especially lenders, in their investing business. These relationships not only generate more leads, and thus more opportunities to buy real estate, but also ensure the very best service when you, the insider, need their services.

My title company was another part of this affiliate partnership. I worked very hard to insert my title company in as many contracts as possible, thereby becoming one of their more active clients. They showed their appreciation by putting my clients' needs at the top of their list and allowed me access to their customer service department, where I could generate leads through hot demographics, both for my clients and for my own investments.

Some of these demographics included people who owned real estate in my town but did not live in my state. These people were in serious need of assistance and mentorship in my area. I formed numerous outstanding relationships with these people, which often resulted in either a listing or a sale of property to me.

Furthermore, in negotiating with clients, my title company would prepare a preliminary title report for me at no charge, allowing me to see the seller's total recorded loans and liens on a property. This gave me an indication of their motivation and ability to sell, and revealed the equity they had in the property. These were all outstanding negotiating tools that normally would not be available to a real estate agent or anyone else because of the cost of producing a preliminary title report.

Another great team member was my termite company. In California, termites are a major deal breaker, and the quality between termite companies can vary immensely. I found the best termite company in the area and observed that they cared about my clients. Thus it was easy for me to involve the company in my transactions. Since I was one of their major lead generators for termite work, they increased their manpower on my personal transactions and sent out their best people; therefore any potential problems had a better chance of being disclosed during my personal contract negotiations.

Home warranty companies can also be outstanding affiliates. In many of my transactions, I negotiated the seller to pay for a home warranty policy. Frequently, there were gray areas in the coverage of systems under the policy. Since I was a major provider of warranties to the company, these gray areas were always resolved in my favor. Once again, my real estate business allowed me insider benefits for my personal transactions.

Accountants, attorneys, insurance providers, home inspectors, and appraisers were other affiliates who gave me extra services because I provided them with business.

Appraisers probably helped me the most. Appraising is an imprecise science, and different appraisers can assign great swings in values. As a business provider to certain appraisers, I received every consideration as they checked and rechecked comparables for values. It was this attention to detail that allowed me to complete many of my transactions.

Being an insider in real estate gives you many opportunities to find people who know about available properties that meet your parameters. The moving company to which I always referred clients knew the area I had targeted for small and inexpensive brick homes and notified me when they received an estimate for moving. Not only was I usually the first person to talk to the owners about a listing, but I also could try to buy the property.

My lender informed me of any buyers who had a property they needed to sell in order to buy a new one. While my lender was prequalifying the borrowers for the new property, the subject of their existing real estate always came up. My lender knew the parameters I was looking for in an investment property and mentioned me to the owners as a possibility for listing their property.

Your other affiliates can also get into the game. There is no reason not to share your investment parameters with the representatives from your home warranty, inspection, contractor, attorney, accountant, escrow company, title company, and all the other companies that you use.

You need to maintain a good relationship with your peers in the area. The real estate agents in my area knew the parameters and the areas of properties that I was looking for. I was part of an investment club in Long Beach, California, where I pitched both my buyers' wants and my wants. On a regular basis, I also used e-mail to send my wants to all the real estate agents on the board. My needs were always posted on my have/want facilities, where I corresponded with the top 10 percent of the Long Beach agents. As the group leader, I would collect the agents' best listings and best buyers every Thursday; then I would assemble the information, including my investment needs, and e-mail it back to the participants.

By building these alliances, I extended my reach to people who were looking for properties that might not be on market yet. Many agents who knew of my needs would call me the moment they took a new listing.

Include your own hopes, wants, and aspirations on all the mediums you use to advertise for your buyers' wants. It is important for the people who make money from your work to understand that the greatest asset they can bring you is a lead on an investment property. This insider advantage is simple: Cultivate the relationships you build every day as additional "bird dogs" and apply the leads you gain to your personal investor business.

CHAPTER 11

More Insider
Investing Tactics

We are getting close to writing an offer on a piece of real estate through the systems we generated from our real estate business and outlined in this book. There are no time restraints and there is no need to rush when looking for a piece of real estate. Because of your insider status, you will be bombarded with hundreds of potential opportunities every day—from your lead generation of sellers, contracts that you negotiate for buyers that do not work out, and sellers who are impatient to find a buyer. Because of this, you must maintain high standards for your investments. However, when found, tie it up quick! The following chapters provide guidelines to verify that the property meets your parameters.

Before we get into the actual writing of contracts, I want to describe some other real estate opportunities that came my way because I was an insider:

• *"If I don't sell your property, I will buy it."* This was one of my advertising promotions as a real estate agent that increased my phone calls from potential sellers. I advertised, in all sincerity, that if I could not sell the property then I would buy it within a certain time frame. I also disclosed the following conditions for this guarantee:

> *The sellers had to list the property at a price that would allow the property to sell. If they were in need of a fast sale through me, they would have to discount the property another 5 percent. Furthermore, I charged my full 6 percent commission. This allowed motivated sellers an opportunity to close the property with me in a 30- to 90-day time period. This was an outstanding way to achieve seller phone calls and meet with sellers to determine their motivations and goals. Occasionally, the seller would take me up on the offer, and I was able to add more property to my inventory.*

• *I made fast turns to my waiting buyers.* Many times, I was introduced to real estate that did not meet my personal investment parameters but there was equity in the property. With full disclosure to all parties so there would be no hard feelings from buyers or sellers, I would purchase these properties and offer them to my buyers with a profit to me. Many times, I could insert myself between a buyer and a seller for a larger piece of the action, not just the commission. This tactic is absolutely legal if everyone understands, with full disclosure, how much I paid and how much I am selling the property for. Surety of close to the seller or rewriting the transaction into a lease option for the buyer—many times I could add value by inserting me (as an inside investor, with full disclosure) into the transaction.

• *I gave seconds.* Another opportunity for insiders is giving *seconds* to buyers. Often, I could negotiate worthwhile transactions that just did not meet my individual parameters. These prenegotiated transactions were easy to turn over to my buyers, who were extremely happy to receive them.

• *I shifted from buyer to lister.* Many times after negotiating a transaction with a seller, I determined that the transaction did not meet my needs, nor my seller's. I was unable to close the transaction, but I could handle the marketing. Who knew more about the property than me?

When you become an insider in your real estate brokerage, you find hundreds of opportunities for investments.

CHAPTER 12

Insider Negotiating

At this point, you have used your insider advantage to find unique properties that no one else may have viewed. You have developed a game plan matching your knowledge of the property to see if it meets your investment goals. All signs point to "go"—now, you must negotiate a contract.

This facet of insider investing in real estate is often the most satisfying and fun. As a real estate agent, you are representing your buyer, or both the buyer and seller to negotiate terms in their best interest. Sometimes, adversarial negotiations can end with a winner and a loser. The most satisfying negotiation for me is when both parties walk away with everything, perhaps even more than they need. Traditionally, this is called a *win-win* negotiation. Since I am my own client, I am in a much better position to make that happen, especially with the knowledge and expertise that I have gained negotiating for so many clients over the years.

I am well aware that the largest number I am going to be dealing with is the purchase price. There is always the possibility of a better price, but price is not the only determination of value. Sometimes, I can get a better price and give the sellers more of what they need. I am all about making checklists. They may not make you the most skilled negotiator, but you can certainly become a better one by using checklists to map out your strategy. Thorough preparation is necessary to achieve a win-win situation.

Putting yourself in the owners' shoes allows you to prepare an offer that meets their needs and exceeds their expectations. To do this, you must find out as much as possible about the sellers. You have to determine the price and the terms that you want; this means determining what the initial offer should be compared with the highest price you are willing to pay. Thinking like a chess player helps you choose the steps of the negotiations that will gradually improve the offer. These moves may end in the highest price that you can pay for the property, but along the way you need to know what the sellers really need so that you can offer other items instead of price.

Prior to the negotiations, I have used the following list to determine what might turn the sellers "on." If allowed access, I would try to talk to the sellers' real estate agent and would call previous negotiators of the sellers as well as the sellers themselves for answers to these questions:

• *How much did they pay for the property?* You can usually find the owners' purchase price by checking the tax records or deeds in the county records. You should always know how much pressure you are going to receive from an offer. If the offer is close to the original purchase price, the sellers may actually be losing money because of the costs of commissions and closing. Rather than frustrating the owners, you may want to initially offer a higher face-saving price.

• *What is the balance of all the mortgages and liens?* From the mortgage balance, you can estimate the owners' gross proceeds after settlement. Since the sellers will be calculating the number every time an offer is presented, it will be smart for you to find out how they perceive these offers.

• *Are there any unrecorded liens or other undisclosed liens that need to be paid?* Once again, it is smart to know what the sellers will be receiving in net proceeds.

• *After the sale, what do the sellers plan to do with the proceeds?* This is an important question because sometimes you can show them faster ways to receive what they are seeking. You might be able to provide a higher interest rate than they could get themselves, or possibly you could provide the same or better asset with the proceeds. This will also suggest whether different kinds of financing on the property might meet the sellers' needs better than institutional financing.

• *What were the hot points and sticking points in any previous negotiations with these sellers?* If you can find the sellers' previous negotiators (check the county's registry of deeds) and ask the listing agent for some insight, you may avoid these problems and endear yourself to the sellers. Once you understand their negotiating style, you may know exactly what low-cost or high-value arrangement might please the sellers.

• *Ask about the sellers' tax situation, tax bracket, and any other information such as 1031 tax deferred exchange deadlines.* By asking questions about employment and lifestyle, you can make an educated guess about the sellers' income level. Since selling a property without taking tax information into consideration can greatly increase a person's tax bracket or at best be a major taxing event, it might be important to structure or negotiate terms that will best help the sellers. Knowing the sellers' depreciation and recapture will also be important. Tax laws governing real estate have numerous deadlines; these requirements, if met, can save sellers tens of thousands of dollars, allowing you to do a better job for them while achieving your goals.

• *Make a prioritized list of "throw away" items.* These are the selling points that you will negotiate initially then concede in order of importance. This approach allows you to make many concessions that are not important to you, but could be important to a seller. They are evidence of your cooperation in trying to achieve the seller's goals; leave more important items as the last and the hardest things to negotiate away. I write down numerous items that I would like to see included, in order of least important to most important.

Prior to negotiation, I always determine the following items:

- The initial higher price and terms
- The target price and terms
- The worst price and terms

I write down this information so that I do not become emotional during negotiations. Emotions cause sellers to dig their heels into the sand, frustrating what the negotiator is trying to accomplish for both parties. Documentation helps deter the emotional storms that accompany all important negotiations. Because I plan carefully before the negotiation process, I am usually the best-prepared negotiator at the table.

Being at the table brings up a good point—many times, the listed agent, as proxy, will present an offer to the sellers. As a trained negotiator, I recommend that the sellers, their own representative, and you should be present at the negotiations, if at all possible. By being present at a negotiation, you can see what bothers the sellers and what items are easy concessions. This will allow you to prioritize items that will encourage the seller to help you achieve your goals. With the listing agent acting as an mediator between you and the seller, you cannot identify the fine points of the negotiation that will allow you to give wins to the seller, while meeting your goals. Always try to be present during the negotiations. As an agent, I always try to do that for my buyers. Remember, you are your own most important client.

Prior to negotiating a transaction, you need to know the exact terms. If the existing promissory note is not available for your approval, it might be in the best interest of you and the sellers to determine whether this lien can be taken over at a favorable rate. Next, I send my loan questionnaire to the lender to allow me to make a better determination about financing (see Form 12.1).

During a negotiation, the information you acquire from research is more trustworthy than what the seller says. Form 12.2 shows the insider financing checklist I have developed over my many years of negotiating loans for my clients. If I have to apply for a new loan, I want to understand it for myself; remember it is more important to achieve the right terms than the right price. The answers to the questions on Form 12.2 allow me to properly compare available new loans, if necessary.

After you have determined the sellers' needs and the potential of the underlying loans, you can start thinking about preparing an offer. Your offer can be as simple as a letter of intent that spells out the basics of an offer subject to the approval of all parties of the final documents. I like to present my offer with all the terms and conditions up front and available for everyone to talk about. Because I have done my homework and know I want the property in question, I use the agreement of sale checklist shown in Form 12.3 to determine that I am using the right insider power in my offer. Real estate organizations tend to use generic real estate contracts that may differ greatly in content. I have always been a believer in using the most commonly accepted contract in my geographic area because that seems to make most real estate agents much more comfortable. Since contracts vary greatly from state to state, always make certain that you have included all essential clauses. This checklist will ensure that you implement the necessary clauses.

I have developed some insider clauses for my own investments as well as the investments of my clients. They serve to clarify the transaction, which can be muddied by fiduciary duties, and are offered in the spirit of full disclosure. The following disclosures are in no particular order:

- *Included in the purchase price are:*
  - —Tenants' deposits and written rental agreements, which will pass to the purchaser through escrow.
  - —All personal property of seller currently used for the benefit of the property and/or the tenants; seller to provide an inventory and bill of sale of same through escrow (by way of illustration, but not of limitation: carpets, rugs, and floor coverings; drapes, curtains, shades, and window coverings; built-in and freestanding appliances; all light fixtures, hanging and wall-affixed, gardening tools and equipment, etc.).
  - —Oil, gas, mineral rights and leases, unless previously reserved of record.
- *Condition of the premises:*
  - —Seller shall maintain premises in current condition through close of escrow.
  - —All systems (e.g., but not of limitation: water, gas, plumbing, electrical, heating, and cooling) to be operable at close of escrow (water heaters and built-in appliances shall be considered to be a part of the plumbing and/or electrical systems) and roof to be watertight; buyer shall have a walk-through inspection within _____ days prior to close of escrow to determine same.
  - —Seller warrants that there are no undisclosed defects in either premises or title.
- *Agreements:* Seller will not enter into any agreement longer than month-to-month with either tenants or vendors pending close of escrow; seller warrants that there are no undisclosed agreements with tenants.
- *Internal Revenue Code (IRC) Section 1031 Exchange:* If seller wishes to participate in an IRC Section 1031 Tax Deferred Exchange, buyer will cooperate with seller's exchange, at no additional cost to buyer. However, this transaction shall close regardless of seller's ability to close his exchange.
- *Inspections:* Buyer shall have the right to inspect and approve:
  - —The interior and exterior of all structures on the premises.
  - —The books and records relating to the ownership and operation of the property for the past 24 months.

—The notes, encumbrances, and security devices to which the property is subject, unless buyer is not going to assume same or take the property subject thereto.

—These inspections are to take place within _____ days of the acceptance of this offer and any counteroffers thereto; seller shall make the property and all of the above items available to buyer or buyer's authorized agent; the period for inspections shall be extended for the number of days seller takes to provide the above-mentioned items should the above-mentioned deadline not be met by seller.

—Escrow shall not open until all inspections have been made and approval given; deposit of signed escrow instructions shall remove these contingencies about inspections and approvals only; any other contingencies shall be dealt with independently of this provision regarding "inspections."

—Buyer acknowledges that Buyer is responsible for making a thorough inspection of the subject property at Buyer's expense, as well as thoroughly researching any information available about the property and its surroundings. It is recommended by Sanford Systems that Buyer obtain a general inspection and written report from a licensed inspection company and a separate written report from specialists, if recommended by the general inspector, or if there is concern on the part of Buyer. Buyer should obtain written cost quotations for all work recommended so as to be fully aware of the potential costs of repairs, maintenance, improvements, and/or upgrades that may be needed. Buyer certifies that Buyer has not relied upon any representations, opinions, or statements made by Seller, Sanford Systems, _____, or any of their agents with regard to the condition of the property or possible violations under city, county, or other governmental agency regulations. It is further understood by Buyer and Seller that Sanford Systems and _____ or any of their agents are not experts in construction and are not too familiar with the condition of the property since they have not resided in the premises. Seller shall make premises available for all inspections. Buyer to keep property free and clear of any liens, indemnify and hold Seller harmless from all liability, claims, demands, damage, or cost and repair all damages to the property arising from the inspection.

• *Referrals:* Buyer and Seller acknowledge that any recommendations concerning referrals to service and vendors including, without limitations, lending institutions, loan brokers, title insurers, escrow companies, inspectors, pest control operators, contractors, repairmen, and the like, are based on the following disclosures: (a) many companies operate in the particular field; (b) costs and quality of product or service may vary; (c) any referral or recommendation is based on Broker's past experience and future performance cannot be guaranteed; (d) Buyer and Seller are free to select services or vendors other than those referred or recommended by Broker, and (e) Buyer and Seller agree to indemnify and hold harmless Broker from claims, disputes, or actions relating to the choice of companies or vendors providing products or services as described above.

• *Walk-through:* Buyer to have a walk-through of subject property at opening of escrow to ascertain that all plumbing, heating, electrical, air conditioning, and appliances are in working order. The final walk-through shall be for the purpose of determining only that (a) the property has not materially deteriorated prior to close of escrow, and (b) corrective work, if any, to be performed by Seller, has been completed. There will be no further requests honored by seller for buyer besides (a) and (b) above.

• *Verifications:* It is the responsibility of Buyer to verify the square footage of all buildings. Income and expense information supplied by Broker was obtained from Seller and has not been verified independently by Broker. Buyer shall be solely responsible for verifying such information. Estimates or projections of income, gains, or tax benefits supplied by Broker are provided for illustrative purposes only and Broker has no liability if actual results vary. Sanford Systems and its agents are indemnified and held harmless by both Buyer and Seller with regard to said information.

• *Indemnification:* This agreement provides for the Broker to be indemnified and held harmless from the following: (a) any claims for personal injury, property damage, or loss in value of the property arising from or related to the physical condition of the property including, without limitation, any soils, structural, or design problems; (b) any claims or action arising from or due to any inaccuracy in the Disclosure Statement; (c) any actions concerning the verification of items in any paragraph of this addendum or the Real Estate Purchase Contract; (d) any dispute or action concerning or arising from Buyer's decision to purchase said property; (e) any claims, disputes, or actions relating to the choice of companies or vendors providing products or services relating to the inspection, financing, or purchase of said property; (f) any responsibility for the completion of repairs to the subject property, including but not limited to structural pest control work; and (g) any and all costs and expenses, including reasonable attorney's fees and costs suffered or incurred in connection with any of the above matters of indemnification.

• *Breaching party:* If either party breaches this contract, the breaching party will pay all costs incurred, including but not limited to, escrow, title, loan charges, and brokerage fee.

• *Brokerage fee:* Seller hereby irrevocably assigns to the Broker(s) herein, in cash, the commission set forth in the commission agreement set forth in the Real Estate Purchase Contract and Receipt for Deposit. This assignment provides for the disbursement of said commission to Broker(s) by escrow. Escrow commission instructions may not be amended or revoked without the written consent of the Broker(s) herein.

• *Financial statement:* Sellers are to be supplied with a financial statement and two years' tax returns plus current Profit and Loss statement from buyers within three days of acceptance of this agreement. Sellers are to have three days from receipt of said financial statements by sellers' agent to either approve or disapprove of the above financial statements, Profit and Loss, and tax returns in writing. If Sellers disapprove any of the Buyer's financial documents, this agreement will be terminated and all deposits will be returned to the purchaser.

• *Credit:* Sellers are to be supplied with a hard copy of Buyer's credit report within _____ days of acceptance or offer is void. Sellers to have _____ days from receipt of report to either approve or disapprove. If Sellers disapprove Buyer's credit report, this agreement will be terminated and all deposits will be returned to purchaser.

• *Seventy-two hours:* Seller shall have the right to continue to offer the herein property for sale. Should Seller receive an acceptable written offer, then Buyer shall be given written notice of such offer by delivery of said notice to Buyer's agent's office. In the event buyer will not waive the condition to sell his or her house in writing within seventy-two hours from time of delivery to sales agent's office, then this agreement shall be terminated and all deposits will be returned to purchaser. If Buyers do waive the condition to sell their property then buyer must double his or her deposit and prove the existence of enough down payment and credit abilities in writing to close escrow, in escrow within forty-eight hours or void their offer.

• *Multiple offers:* Buyers have been alerted to the fact there have been counteroffers given. Buyer has until _____ o'clock _____ A.M. _____ P.M. to accept. Should more than one counteroffer be accepted. Seller reserves the right to select the offer of his choice and to indicate acceptance by countersigning the one selected. Countersigning is considered Seller's final ratification of accepted offer. In the event another offer is received (prior to the above indicated time and date), it will be considered with the outstanding offers.

• *"Backup" provision:* Buyer hereby acknowledges that Seller has executed a contract(s) to sell the subject property to a third party. Buyer and Seller understand and agree that this offer is a Backup offer subject to the failure of prior offer(s). In the event existing third-party contract(s) having priority become null and void, this contract will become primary ONLY upon written notification from Seller to Buyer. Times for performance under this contract are to commence upon such notification. Until such time as Buyer receives such notification from Seller, Buyer, may, without penalty, withdraw this backup offer and have all deposit monies returned.

• *Short sale/notice of default:* This transaction is contingent upon the lien holders involved in this transaction discounting the amounts due to cooperate with a closing and transfer of ownership. It is also subject to the lien holders reporting the credit aspects of this transaction in a manner acceptable to the seller. It is now fully disclosed that there is, or may be, a Notice of Default filed.

• *Representation:* No representation is made as to the legal validity of any provision or the adequacy of any provision in any specific transaction. A real estate broker is a person qualified to advise on real estate and on business transactions. If you desire legal advice, consult your attorney.

These clauses not only reflected my insider advantages of having negotiated numerous transactions for buyers and sellers, but also were extremely useful when I was making offers for myself. They spell out conditions clearly in areas that are most often litigated in a transaction, and they also help prove that you have the sellers' best interest in mind. Finally, I like to offer sellers some facts about their buyer so that they feel more confident about my offer, which in their mind is coming from an insider, and causing them trepidation. Form 12.4, "Facts about Your Buyer," can be attached as the last page of your offer.

During the negotiations, I often find that the listing agent has neglected to provide and explain to the owners what their net proceeds will be. I am always prepared to do this for sellers, even though I do not represent them. One of the advantages of being an insider is that I can think for both sides.

Form 12.5 is my standard seller's net sheet or net estimated proceeds of the seller's exchange for a piece of real estate. It is all-inclusive and easy to understand.

The next insider document you should reach for is your well-read, state-approved real estate purchase contract. Many real estate contract forms are available; however, using the one that is most familiar in your area will make it easier for the sellers' representative to explain the terms to them. This can save you much pain.

Now that the negotiations are proceeding on a basis of solving the sellers' needs and you have done an outstanding job of determining those needs, it is time to use your insider advantage and not get emotionally involved in this piece of real estate. As an insider, you get to look at opportunities every day.

Another advantage of being an insider during these negotiations is that you may negotiate an outstanding contract, but decide it is not quite good enough to meet your personal investment parameters. When a counterproposal comes back that won't allow you to buy the property, research your database to see which of your buyers will be perfect for this prenegotiated opportunity. As an insider, I negotiated contracts that I was unwilling to close on and used them as inventory for my buyer database. In my correspondence to agents in my database, I let them know about this opportunity and always had a list of ready, willing, and able real estate investors who were ready to step into my shoes when I was unwilling or unable to close. If I knew that I could find a buyer, I would write the following: "Walter Sanford and/or assignee identified prior to close."

Real estate is a game where everyone can win when you keep your options open and care about the people you are dealing with.

Downloadable FORM 12.1
Loan Questionnaire*

Name
Company
Address
City, ST Zip

Name:

The property at (property address) is now on the market for sale. To clear up any confusion regarding the existing loan on (property address), the loan number is (insert loan number). I would appreciate your assurances on the following loan terms. Please be advised that I will keep you informed every step of the way should a buyer wish to assume this loan.

1. Payment Amount

What is it?   _____

How often can it change? _____

Is there a limit on how much it can change (over a one-year period and/or over total life of loan)? _____

Are there exceptions to that limit? _____

2. Note Rate

What is it?   _____

How often can it change? _____

What index is the change based on? _____

What is the spread (also called margin) between the note rate and the index?
_____

Is there a limit to how high and low the note rate can go? _____

Are there exceptions to that limit? _____

3. Negative Amortization
Is negative amortization possible under the terms of this loan? _____

If so, how often is it added to the principal balance? _____

What is done if negative amortization grows too large? _____

4. Assumability

Is this an assumable loan? _____

Is there a "due-on-sale" clause in the note? _____

*Copyright © 2006 by Walter Sanford. To customize this document, download to your hard drive from www.waltersanford .com/insiderinvestingforms. The document can then be opened, edited, and printed using Microsoft Word or another popular word processing application.

5. Current owner of the loan _____

6. Contact Name from the Bank _____

7. Telephone number _____

   E-mail _____

8. Number of years left on the loan _____

9. Points to assume _____

10. All fees to assume

    A. _____ B. _____ C. _____

    D. _____ E. _____ F. _____

11. Estimated approval time _____

12. Approximate principal balance of loan $ _____

Thank you so much for your help.

Sincerely,

Seller/Listing Agent
Company

Borrowers/Owners consent to release information to (insert your name):

_____

_____

Borrower/Buyer:_____ Date: _____

Borrower/Buyer:_____ Date: _____

Downloadable FORM 12.2
Insider Financing Checklist*

1. Discount fee (points)_____

2. Prepayment penalty terms, if any_____

3. Mortgage assumption option, if any _____

4. Garbage fees for drawing papers_____

5. Appraisal fees _____

6. Interest rate: fixed or variable _____

7. If variable: Index _____   Max _____

             Margin _____   Min_____

8. Assignment fee, if appropriate_____

9. Length of commitment period _____

10. Balloon payments, if any_____

11. Size and number of escrow or impound accounts required at settlement
and monthly payments_____

12. Other fees _____

13. Personal liability clause _____

14. What does the lender require regarding:
   A. Fire insurance _____
   B. Title insurance _____
   C. Survey _____
   D. Termite inspection and certification _____
   E. Flood insurance _____
   F. Mortgage insurance premium _____
   G. Subordination clause _____

Additional Notes on Financing

_____

_____

_____

_____

_____

_____

_____

_____

_____

_____

*Copyright © 2006 by Walter Sanford. To customize this document, download to your hard drive from www.waltersanford .com/insiderinvestingforms. The document can then be opened, edited, and printed using Microsoft Word or another popular word processing application.

Agreement of Sale Checklist*

1. Mortgage contingency clause _____

_____

_____

_____

_____

This specifies not only the mortgage amount but also the term, interest rate, monthly payment, and maximum prepayment penalty.

2. Date and location of closing _____

_____

_____

3. Termite certification (method) _____

_____

_____

4. Clear title (insurable) _____

_____

_____

5. Type of deed and method of holding title _____

_____

_____

6. Identity of holder of deposit _____

_____

_____

7. Prohibition against the seller entering into new, adverse leases _____

_____

_____

8. Estoppel certificates from tenants _____

_____

_____

9. Prorated expenses, taxes, rents, insurance, and interest on security deposits _____

_____

_____

10. Transfer of security deposits _____

_____

_____

*Copyright © 2006 by Walter Sanford. To customize this document, download to your hard drive from www.waltersanford.com/insiderinvestingforms. The document can then be opened, edited, and printed using Microsoft Word or another popular word processing application.

(continued)

11. All personal property which is included in tenants' rent that is to be included in the sale (furniture, refrigerators, throw rugs, etc.) _____

_____

_____

12. Remedies if either party cancels without cause _____

_____

_____

13. Warranty that present use is legal _____

_____

_____

Verify this by a letter to the local zoning board after signing of the agreement.

14. Verify soil hazards _____

_____

_____

15. Date possession is to be given _____

16. Designation of who pays which fees—buyer or seller _____

_____

_____

17. Disclosure of whether either party holds a real estate license (such disclosure is usually required by state law) _____

_____

_____

18. Permission to make a presettlement inspection and what is covered _____

_____

_____

19. Warranties of the rent schedule and terms of leases _____

_____

_____

20. Warranty that seller has received no notices of violations of the housing codes _____

_____

_____

21. Permission to inspect all apartments if that has not been done prior to signing of the agreement of sale _____

22. Copies of all leases whether tenant-signed or owner-signed _____

23. The following items should be checked at the presettlement inspection:

    A. Personal property that is included or excluded from the sale, such as drapes, light fixtures, and appliances _____

_____

    B. Condition of the premises at the time the property change hands (e.g., "broom clean") _____

_____

_____

    C. Property damage that will void the sale _____

    D. Warranty that the plumbing, heating, and electrical systems are in working order at settlement _____

    E. 1031 Tax Deferred Exchange contingency _____

Additional Notes on Agreement of Sale

_____

_____

_____

_____

_____

_____

_____

_____

_____

Downloadable FORM 12.4
Facts about Your Buyer*

Have the buyers been prequalified? _____ Yes   _____ No

What lender has prequalified them: _____

_____

Loan Rep: _____

Phone number: _____ E-mail: _____

For what amount are they qualified: _____

_____

_____

What interest rates were used for qualifying: _____

Is this a single or dual income: _____

How long with present employer? _____

Has credit report been run?   _____ Yes   _____ No

Please include written report only with Buyer's approval.

Any challenges?   _____Yes   _____ No

Any contingencies?   _____ Yes   _____ No

Can we easily verify:

    Employment?   _____ Yes   _____ No

    Deposit?   _____ Yes   _____ No

    Existing Mortgages?   _____ Yes   _____ No

    Down payments?   _____ Yes   _____ No

    Closing costs?   _____ Yes   _____ No

How? _____

_____

_____

_____

Reason for purchasing: _____

_____

_____

_____

_____

*Copyright © 2006 by Walter Sanford. To customize this document, download to your hard drive from www.waltersanford .com/insiderinvestingforms. The document can then be opened, edited, and printed using Microsoft Word or another popular word processing application.

Plans for existing tenants: _____

_____

_____

_____

Plans for this property: _____

_____

_____

_____

_____   _____
             Buyer   Lender

_____   _____
          Print Name   Print Name

Downloadable FORM 12.5

Seller's Net Sheet: Estimated Proceeds on Sale or Exchange of Property*

The amounts estimated in this net sheet are for the following agreement:	
❏ Deposit receipt ❏ Counteroffer ❏ Exchange agreement ❏ Seller's listing agreement ❏ Escrow instructions Dated: _____, 20 _____ Entered into by: _____	Prepared for: _____ Prepared by: _____ Dated prepared: _____, 20 _____ Closing date anticipated: _____, 20 _____ Property Sold/Exchanged: _____

Sales Price		**Adjustment to Net Equity for Prorates**	
1. Price received		27. **Estimated Net Equity** (Carried forward)	$ _____
Add:	$ _____		
Encumbrances		**Prorates Due Buyer**	
2. First Trust Deed	$ _____	28. Rent Collected and Unearned at Close	$ _____
3. Second Trust Deed	$ _____	29. Tenant Deposits	$ _____
4. Other Encumbrances/ Liens	$ _____	30. Unpaid Property Taxes	$ _____
5. **Total Encumbrances**		31. Accrued Interest Unpaid	$ _____
Deduct:	$ _____	32. **Total** Prorates Due Buyer	
6. Title Insurance Premium	$ _____	**Deduct:**	$ _____
7. Escrow Fees	$ _____	33. Prepaid Property Taxes	$ _____
8. Notary Fees	$ _____	34. Prepaid Insurance Premium	$ _____
9. Document Preparation Fee	$ _____	35. Impound Account Balance	$ _____
10. Documentary Transfer Taxes	$ _____	36. Prepaid Homeowner's Assessment	$ _____
11. Recording Fees	$ _____	37. Prepaid Ground Lease	$ _____
12. Home Warranty Premium	$ _____	38. Prepaid Equipment Lease	$ _____
13. Homeowner's Statement Fees	$ _____	39. **Total** Pro-Rations Due Seller **Add:**	$ _____
14. Pest Control Report	$ _____	40. **Estimated Proceeds at Closing:**	$ _____
15. Pest Control Repairs (Approx.)	$ _____		
16. Prepayment Penalties	$ _____		

*Copyright © 2006 by Walter Sanford. To customize this document, download to your hard drive from www.waltersanford .com/insiderinvestingforms. The document can then be opened, edited, and printed using Microsoft Word or another popular word processing application.

Downloadable FORM 12.5   *(Continued)*

17. Smoke Detector	$ _____	The net proceeds from sale/exchange will be in the form of:
18. Re-conveyance Fees	$ _____	Cash $ _____
19. Beneficiary Statement Fee	$ _____	Note secured by carry back trust deed. $ _____
20. FHA-VA loan Appraisal Fee	$ _____	Other:
21. FHA-VA Points (Approx.____%)	$ _____	_____
22. Repairs Rqrd. by Lender (Approx.)	$ _____	
23. Brokerage Fee	$ _____	This net sheet assists the seller to anticipate net proceeds at close and in what form these proceeds will be received. The figures estimated in this net sheet may vary and thus cannot be guaranteed because of daily changes in lender demands, escrow fees, other charges, and prorates. Tax consequences are not included in this form.
24. Attorney's Fee	$ _____	
25. Accountant's Fee	$ _____	
26. **Total** Sales Expenses and Charges **Deduct:**	$ _____	
27. **Estimated Net Equity**	$ _____	

Seller's Agent: _____	I have received and read a copy of this estimate of net proceeds.
Address: _____	Seller's Name: _____
_____	Address: _____
E-mail: _____	_____
Phone: _____	E-mail: _____
Date: _____, 20 _____	Phone: _____
Agent's Signature: _____	Seller's Signature: _____
	Seller's Signature: _____
	Date: _____, 20 _____

CHAPTER 13

Doing the Due Diligence as Only an Insider Can

Doing your insider diligence means it is crunch time. You have well-conceived *weasel* clauses in your contract that will allow you to extricate yourself from the transaction if you find anything wrong with the property. You have already made a brief inspection by driving by and reviewing the paperwork that the listing agent or seller has given you, and you have made an initial judgment whether this property is going to fit your needs. This information was further bolstered by the information you received from the seller and the listing agent during the contract process.

Now, it is time to make a thorough inspection. You should use the team that you know best. You have made many affiliates successful by introducing them to your buyers; now it is time for them to pay you back with due diligence to make certain that the transaction meets all your needs.

On any inspection, bring in a professional inspector; specialized heating, ventilation, and air conditioning (HVAC) contractors; and licensed termite/pest inspectors. Your insider status should allow you to get the most highly qualified professionals at a moment's notice. The inspection should take as long as needed for all personnel to cover the property completely. Try to have all inspectors there during the same time frame to minimize the inconvenience to tenants. It is imperative that you get into *all* areas in each room so you can put together an all-inclusive list. Bring the sellers a complete list at the outset because small requests spread over time will be an annoyance to them.

Over my many years of being a real estate broker, I have developed a kit that helps my inspectors or clients inspect the properties more effectively. I have learned that a building inspection cannot be left to the human eye. Parts of the structure may only be accessible or visible if you have the right tools. Form 13.1 is a checklist that helps you have everything ready to determine the quality of the property that you are about to buy. Multiple inspections irritate everyone—sellers, tenants, inspectors, and buyers. I put this kit together with the goal of achieving a one-shot inspection while capturing every problem that should be negotiated prior to close.

After you have assembled the inspection kit, prepare your inspection checklist. Form 13.2 is the building inspection checklist that I created for my clients. An insider's advantage is that you can use your best client-pleasing tools for yourself. As with everything in this book—if it was good enough for them, then it was good enough for me.

After completing your inspection, your next priority is finding out about the tenants you are about to inherit. Tenants can make or break a transaction and are the key to the profit or pain you will receive on any investment. If I have learned anything from my thousands of clients, it is that spending a little time with tenants *before* the purchase can save me many headaches after the purchase.

Tenant interviews are extremely important in any thorough assessment of an investment. They are intimately familiar with a property and frequently believe that complaining to outsiders—especially prospective buyers—will force their landlord to solve the problems. Some tenants may also try to sabotage the sale if the seller has aggressively raised the rents or failed to meet their maintenance expectations. Tenants rarely try to conceal defects from a buyer. If they do, they probably enjoy low rent or something makes them loyal to the seller. Form 13.3 lists some questions that will help you identify any potential problems.

Take a copy of Form 13.3 with you when you inspect the building. You are likely to see some of the tenants as you visit apartments, and when you do, ask them if they would mind answering a few questions. Do not let the real estate agent or owners talk you out of speaking with tenants. If you don't encounter any tenants during your inspection, go back later (subject to your agreement with the seller). Even the most thorough, experienced inspector can easily overlook problems known to every tenant in the building. Tenants are an *excellent* source of information on a prospective acquisition.

Even though interviews are helpful, it is essential to rely on written records. In your contract, include tenant estoppel agreements to be signed by the tenants prior to close. Form 13.4 is a copy of my tenant estoppel statement, which prevents tenants from making verbal claims at a later date. Remember, in real estate—it does not count unless it is in writing.

Last, request source records of all expenses. I like to have copies of Schedule E for the preceding two years and all the supporting documents necessary to prove the figures on the schedule. Often, Schedule E will not match the actual operating statements of the building, but if the owners are selling the property on numbers other than the ones on that schedule, they must prove those numbers for you. They may be cheating on their income taxes, but there is no need for you to pass up a good transaction if they have proof of the expenses. Do the same due diligence that you would do for a client. *You are your own best client* and you need to use your insider experience to get the facts on this building that you are about to live with.

One of the next pieces of due diligence that I perform is a market rent survey. Form 13.5 shows the survey I use to list the competing properties in the neighborhood and determine where my rent should be.

After collecting all this information, it is time to take a deep breath and start evaluating whether this property is really the transaction for you.

Downloadable FORM 13.1

Inspection Kit*

❑ Digital camera with flash, an extra memory card, and batteries

Photographic equipment can provide material for your mortgage application, help you remember various aspects of a building after the inspection, and prove your negotiations to the seller.

❑ Binoculars

Binoculars enable you to inspect some roofs and the upper exterior of the building without climbing a ladder.

❑ Ice pick/probe

An ice pick is used to check for termites and dry rot. Unless you are an expert, you should also have a licensed termite inspector check the property.

❑ Utility light and extension cord

❑ Flashlight

These items permit you to inspect the dark sections of basements, crawl spaces, and attics.

❑ 100-foot tape measure

❑ Stud finder

❑ Level

❑ A round marble

This is used to determine sloping floors; basement floors should slope toward the drain.

❑ Multihead screwdriver

❑ Pliers

❑ Claw hammer

These tools will help you open access panels and stuck doors. Always get the owner's permission.

❑ Overalls

❑ Painter's hat

❑ Baby wipes

It is virtually impossible to make a thorough inspection without getting dirty.

❑ Clipboard, pencil, paper, and calculator

❑ Building inspection checklists

You may want to purchase a toolbox or bag to carry these things in your trunk.

Notes and additional items you want to take:

_____

_____

_____

_____

*Copyright © 2006 by Walter Sanford. To customize this document, download to your hard drive from www.waltersanford .com/insiderinvestingforms. The document can then be opened, edited, and printed using Microsoft Word or another popular word processing application.

Downloadable FORM 13.2
Building Inspection Checklist*

Exterior
Landscaping—describe condition, improvement potential, and general observations about the following:

Lawn _____

_____

_____

_____

Trees _____

_____

_____

_____

Shrubs _____

_____

_____

_____

Paved areas—describe condition, remaining life, appearance of surface, and painted lines on the following:

Parking areas _____

_____

_____

_____

_____

Sidewalks _____

_____

_____

_____

*Copyright © 2006 by Walter Sanford. To customize this document, download to your hard drive from www.waltersanford.com/insiderinvestingforms. The document can then be opened, edited, and printed using Microsoft Word or another popular word processing application.

Downloadable FORM 13.2   *(Continued)*

Driveway _____

_____

_____

Patios/Decks _____

_____

_____

Basketball court _____

_____

_____

Number of stories in the building: _____

Number of wires attached to the building: _____
Two wires indicate an old system; three wires indicate a modern or rewired one.

Evidence of new water service: _____
A rectangular patch about two feet by four feet in the street in front of the building usually means that a new pipe has been laid from the water main to the building. The cut-off stub of the old pipe will also be visible in the basement. New water service is desirable in old properties.

Major bulges along exterior walls: _____

_____

_____

Exterior pipes: _____

_____

_____

These may be subject to freezing in cold weather.

Chimney snug against wall? _____

The chimney will not draw properly if it is below a nearby roof peak.

Sign _____

_____

_____

(continued)

Is there a sign advertising the apartments? Condition, wording, potential?

Lighting _____

_____

_____

_____

Describe appearance, adequacy, and possible improvements in lighting. Visit the property after dark in addition to the normal daylight inspection. Can some fixtures be eliminated, be placed on timers, or wattage reduced? Tenant safety is a concern.

Porch _____

_____

_____

_____

Note the size, condition, and improvement potential. A sagging porch makes a building look as though it is about to collapse, but a porch can usually be repaired with relatively little expense because it is not a part of the main structure.

Noise pollution _____

_____

_____

_____

Visible smoke pollution _____

_____

_____

_____

Odors _____

_____

_____

_____

Excessive traffic _____

_____

_____

These items relate to the general area around the property. Factories and freeways can drastically reduce values if they cause any of these problems. A normally quiet street that is a commuter shortcut twice a day can also create trouble. Check traffic flows at different times of the day.

Are there storm windows on each window, if applicable? _____

Are there screens on each window? _____

The high cost of energy in most parts of the country makes it essential to include either storm windows or thermal sash on your windows. Many state laws require landlords to provide screens on all windows.

Corner or an inside lot? _____

Apparent size and shape of lot? _____

Corner lots are *not* more valuable than other lots. Do not rely on estimates of the lot dimensions. You should have a licensed surveyor provide you with a survey prior to settlement.

Parking:

Number of cars: _____

Covered: _____

Uncovered: _____

Heated (in regions with very cold climates): _____

Check local laws on parking if the property does not have sufficient parking for all tenants.

Roofs:

Types: _____

_____

_____

_____

Estimated remaining life of each: _____

(continued)

Rain gutters and downspouts:

Type: _____

Condition: _____

_____

Be sure to account for all the necessary gutters and downspouts. I have seen entire sides missing!

Painted surfaces: _____

_____

_____

_____

Note condition, remaining life, choice of color, number of coats needed to cover present paint, if poor choice, and amount of time needed for detail work. Current regulations may limit your options if you need to strip off old paint due to lead regulations.

Wrought iron rusted? _____

Mailboxes:

Type: _____

Material: _____

Condition: _____

Intercoms:

Appearance: _____

Do they work? _____

Remote door opener in working order? _____

Doors:

Style: _____

Condition: _____

Hardware appearance and type: _____

Potential for improvement: _____

_____

_____

A little work to improve the appearance of exterior doors can make a building look much better.

Fence:

Condition (check for rot or rust): _____

_____

_____

_____

Appearance: _____

_____

_____

_____

Appropriate for location and architecture of structure: _____

_____

_____

_____

Siding:

Appearance: _____

_____

_____

Condition: _____

_____

_____

Type: _____

_____

_____

Is it hiding a nightmare? _____

Shutters:

Condition: _____

Any missing? _____

(continued)

Downloadable FORM 13.2   *(Continued)*

Fire escapes:

Appearance: _____

_____

_____

_____

Any missing where required? (Usually third floor and above) _____

_____

_____

_____

Exterior access to basement: _____

_____

_____

_____

Refuse removal:

Type: _____

_____

_____

_____

Location: _____

_____

_____

_____

Living Room
(Make more copies for all interior rooms.)

Dimensions: _____

Walls:

Type: _____

Check plumb: _____

Condition: _____

_____

_____

_____

Ceiling:

Type (acoustic tile? plaster?): _____

_____

_____

_____

Condition (falling down? sound? stained?): _____

_____

_____

_____

Height (8'? 10'? etc.): _____

Floor:

Type: _____

_____

_____

_____

(continued)

Downloadable FORM 13.2   *(Continued)*

Condition: _____

_____

_____

_____

Check level: _____

_____

Light switches: _____

_____

_____

Light fixtures: _____

_____

_____

Woodwork:

Finish: _____

_____

_____

Condition: _____

_____

_____

_____

Security peephole or window at entrance: _____

Downloadable FORM 13.2   *(Continued)*

Locks:

Type: _____

_____

_____

_____

Condition: _____

_____

_____

_____

Doors:

Stops on all doors? _____

_____

Check plumb: _____

_____

Enough unbroken wall for a sofa? _____

Heat:

Type: _____

_____

Is it adequate? _____

_____

Thermostat:

Type: _____

_____

Test response time: _____

_____

(continued)

Windows:

Smooth functioning? _____

_____

Type: _____

_____

_____

_____

Condition: _____

_____

_____

_____

Storm windows (all panes intact?): _____

_____

_____

_____

Screens: _____

_____

_____

_____

Drapes:

Type: _____

_____

_____

_____

Condition: _____

_____

_____

_____

Electric outlets (there should be one every 12 feet or so): _____

_____

_____

_____

Additional Notes on Living Room

_____

_____

_____

_____

_____

_____

Kitchen

Dimensions: _____

Walls:

Type: _____

_____

_____

Condition: _____

_____

_____

Check plumb: _____

Ceiling:

Type: _____

_____

_____

Condition: _____

_____

_____

(continued)

Height: _____

Floor:

Type: _____

_____

_____

Condition: _____

_____

_____

Check level: _____

Cabinets:

Type: _____

_____

_____

Condition: _____

_____

_____

Color: _____

All drawers and doors operate properly? _____

_____

_____

Countertop:

Type: _____

_____

_____

Condition: _____

_____

_____

Color: _____

Downloadable FORM 13.2   *(Continued)*

Sink:

Type: _____

_____

Condition: _____

_____

Color: _____

Age: _____

Range:

Type: _____

_____

_____

Condition (inside and out): _____

_____

_____

_____

Size: _____

Color: _____

Age: _____

Refrigerator:

Owned by tenant? _____

Type: _____

_____

_____

Condition: _____

_____

_____

Color: _____

Age: _____

(continued)

Light switches: _____

Light fixtures: _____

_____

Adequate number of outlets? _____

GFCI outlet by sink? _____

Woodwork:

Finish: _____

Condition: _____

Doorstops on all doors? _____

Adequate storage space? _____

_____

Faucets:

Type: _____

_____

Condition: _____

_____

_____

Test for rusty water, temperature, pressure: _____

_____

Water cutoffs? _____

Disposal:

Check make and model: _____

Test operation: _____

Windows:

Smooth functioning? _____

Note which ones, if any, need work: _____

_____

_____

Downloadable FORM 13.2 *(Continued)*

Type: _____

_____

_____

Condition: _____

_____

_____

Storm windows (all panes intact?): _____

_____

Screens: _____

Exhaust fan (smooth functioning?): _____

_____

Range hood:

Light: _____

Self-vented or exterior vent: _____

Exterior door:

Type: _____

Condition: _____

Storm door: _____

Heat:

Type: _____

Adequate: _____

Other appliances:

Type: _____

_____

Condition: _____

_____

Color: _____

(continued)

Additional Notes on Kitchen

_____

_____

_____

_____

_____

_____

Basement, Utility Room, Crawl Space

This phase of your overall inspection should be last to avoid tracking dirt
through the apartments and halls.

Wall:

Type: _____

_____

_____

Condition: _____

_____

_____

Check plumb (not as important as in living space): _____

Evidence of termite treatment? _____

_____

_____

Sill plate damaged by termites or dry rot? _____

_____

_____

Joists:

Size: _____

Spacing: _____

Bridging: _____

Condition: _____

_____

_____

Check for cracks, dry rot, and termites.

Wiring:

Type: _____

_____

Condition: _____

_____

_____

Are there separate meters for each apartment? _____

_____

Plumbing:

Type: _____

_____

_____

Evidence of leaks: _____

Evidence of flooding: _____

_____

Sump pump: _____

Ejector pump: _____

Heating system:

Type: _____

_____

Condition: _____

_____

_____

Age: _____

(continued)

Fuel: _____

Condition of combustion chamber: _____

Type of piping: _____

Blower motor? _____

Pipe insulation? _____

Low water cutoff? _____
A low water cutoff is a safety device that turns off the heater if the amount of water drops below a safe level.

Heater insulated? _____

Evidence of repairs or leaks? _____

_____

Capacity of oil storage tanks, if any: _____

_____

Oil dealer name and number: _____

Support columns:

Type: _____

_____

_____

Condition: _____

_____

_____

Outside door:

Type: _____

_____

_____

Condition: _____

_____

_____

Does it lock? _____

Check plumb: _____

Steps:

Condition: _____

Ceiling:

Height: _____

Fire-resistant material? _____

Electric service panel:

Fuses or circuit breakers? _____

Capacity: _____

Gas meters (one for each apartment?) _____

Water service:

Size: _____

Type of pipe: _____

_____

_____

Water heaters:

Number of units: _____

Capacity in gallons: _____

Type of fuel: _____

Pressure relief valve: _____

Earthquake straps: _____

Air ducts and noise insulation: _____

Drains: _____

Windows:

Type: _____

_____

Do they leak? _____

Crawl space and vapor barrier: _____

(continued)

Bathroom

Floor:

Type: _____

_____

Condition: _____

_____

_____

Check level: _____

Ceiling:

Type: _____

_____

Condition: _____

_____

_____

Walls:

Type: _____

_____

Condition: _____

_____

_____

Check plumb: _____

Toilet:

Condition: _____

_____

_____

Seat: _____

Is the toilet a water-saver model? _____

Age: _____

You can generally find the age of the toilet stamped on the underside of the top of the tank. This is often also the year the building was constructed.

Lavatory sink:

Size: _____

Age: _____

Color: _____

Condition: _____

_____

_____

Vanity: _____

Test water for rust and pressure: _____

Faucets:

Type: _____

_____

Condition: _____

_____

_____

Cutoff valves: _____

Plug: _____

Drain speed: _____

Medicine cabinet:

Size: _____

Tub: _____

Type: _____

_____

Condition: _____

_____

_____

(continued)

Age: _____

Color: _____

Size: _____

Tub wall:

Type: _____

_____

Condition: _____

_____

_____

Type of shower enclosure:

Glass door: _____

Curtain: _____

Shower valve:

Type: _____

_____

Condition: _____

_____

_____

Test hot water for rust and delay time: _____

Test cold water for rust: _____

Drain plug: _____

Drain speed: _____

Shower nozzle:

Type: _____

_____

Condition: _____

_____

_____

Access panel: _____

Type of pipe: _____

_____

Condition: _____

_____

Evidence of leaks: _____

Window:

Type: _____

_____

Smooth functioning? _____

Storm window intact? _____

Screen: _____

Woodwork: _____

Exhaust fan (if no window): _____

Heat: _____

Towel bar: _____

Toilet paper holder: _____

Door:

Type: _____

Condition: _____

_____

Doorstop on door? _____

Lights: _____

GFCI outlet by sink? _____

Additional Notes on Bathrooms

_____

_____

_____

(continued)

Common Areas

Common areas are hallways, lobbies, entries, and most amenities.

Walls:

Type: _____

_____

Check plumb: _____

Condition: _____

_____

Ceiling:

Type: _____

_____

Condition: _____

_____

_____

Floors:

Type: _____

_____

Check level: _____

Condition: _____

_____

_____

Stairways (condition): _____

_____

Handrails: _____

Elevators:

Condition of cab: _____

Dimensions: _____

Are ashtrays available by the elevator on each floor? _____

Where there are no ashtrays for waiting tenants, the floors will be damaged.

Check operation of elevators (use licensed company): _____

_____

Fire extinguishers—inspection current? _____

Mailboxes:

Proper number: _____

Type: _____

_____

Condition: _____

_____

Announcement box: _____

Light fixtures: _____

Fire alarm (if required): _____

Smoke detectors: _____

Doorbells:

Appearance: _____

Operation: _____

Intercom:

Proper functioning of speakers and remote door openers: _____

_____

Appearance: _____

Suggestion box: _____

Additional Notes on Common Areas

_____

_____

_____

_____

_____

(continued)

Bedrooms

Dimensions: _____

Walls:

Type: _____

_____

Check plumb: _____

Condition: _____

_____

_____

Floor:

Type: _____

_____

Check level: _____

Condition: _____

_____

_____

Ceiling:

Type: _____

_____

Condition: _____

_____

_____

Closet space adequate? _____

_____

_____

Will the room accommodate large beds and bureaus? _____

Door:

Type: _____

_____

Check plumb: _____

Condition: _____

_____

_____

Doorstops on all doors? _____

Windows:

Type: _____

_____

Smooth functioning? _____

Storm windows (all panes intact?): _____

_____

Screens: _____

Light fixtures: _____

Light switches: _____

Heat: _____

Woodwork: _____

Adequate number of electric and cable outlets? _____

Additional Notes on Bedrooms

_____

_____

_____

_____

_____

(continued)

Garage

Dimensions: _____

Door:

Does it work properly? _____

Condition: _____

_____

_____

Width adequate? _____

Check plumb on doorjamb: _____

Can it be locked? _____

Roof:

Type: _____

_____

Remaining life (estimated): _____

Walls:

Type: _____

_____

Condition: _____

_____

_____

Check wooden garages for termites or dry rot: _____

_____

Floor:

Type: _____

_____

Condition: _____

_____

_____

Windows intact? (Note any breaks) _____

_____

_____

Any stains on ceiling? _____

_____

Room for overhead storage: _____

_____

_____

Will it pass city garage/storage law? _____

Additional Notes on Garage

_____

_____

_____

_____

_____

_____

Code violations: _____

_____

_____

Detectors: Smoke, fire, radon, heat, infrared, carbon monoxide, water? _____

_____

_____

Downloadable FORM 13.3
Tenant Questions Prior to Investment*

What rent do you pay? _____

Have you received any sort of rent adjustment? (e.g., first month's rent free)

_____

Is the heat adequate? _____

Has the heat been interrupted in the past year? _____

Is the air conditioning adequate? _____

Do you find that you blow fuses or circuit breakers at times? _____

Is your water pressure adequate? _____

Does the roof leak? _____

Does the basement flood during wet weather? _____

Are there drainage problems on the property? _____

Are all of your kitchen appliances in good working order? _____

Do your kitchen and bathroom drains work? _____

Does the owner exterminate regularly? _____

Do you intend to renew your lease? _____

Are you satisfied with the manager's performance? _____

Are there any tenants you wish would move? _____

Are there crime problems in the building? _____

Are there crime problems in the neighborhood? _____

Are there any problems with parking or refuse? _____

Is the area noisy? _____

Are there smoke, odor, or traffic problems? _____

Does your intercom and remote door opener work properly? _____

Additional Notes: _____

_____

_____

*Copyright © 2006 by Walter Sanford. To customize this document, download to your hard drive from www.waltersanford .com/insiderinvestingforms. The document can then be opened, edited, and printed using Microsoft Word or another popular word processing application.

Downloadable FORM 13.4

Tenancy Estoppel Statement

Tenant: _____

Premises: _____

To: _____

Attn: _____ .

To whom it may concern:

1. The undersigned is the Tenant of the above premises, and is currently under the following agreement:

   Lease on address: _____

   Date of the Lease: _____

   Name of the original Landlord: _____

   Name of the original Tenant: _____

   Current monthly base rent: $_____ paid through _____

   Security deposit: $_____ Other deposits: $_____

   Expiration date of current lease term: _____

   Number and length of remaining options to renew or extend if any:

   _____

2. The tenant represents that the original Lease remains in full force and effect and constitutes the entire agreement between Tenant and Landlord, except for the following modifications, amendments, addendums, assignments, extensions, and/or preferential rights or options to purchase/lease:

   _____

   _____

3. Tenant is the actual occupant and is in possession of the Leased Premises. Tenant has not assigned, transferred, or hypothecated its interest under the Lease. Any construction, buildout, improvements, alterations, or additions to the Premises required under the Lease have been fully completed in accordance with the plans and specifications described in the Lease.

4. All obligations of Landlord under the Lease have been fully performed and Landlord is not in default under any term of the Lease. Tenant has no defenses, offsets, or counterclaims to the payment of rent or other amounts due from Tenant to Landlord under the Lease.

*Copyright © 2006 by Walter Sanford. To customize this document, download to your hard drive from www.waltersanford.com/insiderinvestingforms. The document can then be opened, edited, and printed using Microsoft Word or another popular word processing application.

(continued)

5. Tenant has not been given any free rent, partial rent, rebates, rent abatements, or rent concessions of any kind, except as follows:

_____

_____

6. Tenant has not filed and is not the subject of any filing for bankruptcy or reorganization under federal bankruptcy laws or similar state laws.

7. Tenant represents that Tenant (a) is not in default of the performance of any obligation under the Lessee, (b) has not committed any breach of the Lease, and (c) has not received any notice of default under the Lease that has not been cured.

8. The correct address for notices to Tenant is the Premises above unless otherwise shown below.

9. The person signing below represents that he/she is duly authorized by Tenant to execute this Statement on Tenant's behalf.

10. Tenant understands that: (a) a lender may make a loan secured in whole or part by the Premises and that if it does so, its action will be in material reliance on this Statement, and/or (b) a buyer may acquire the Premises or the building in which the Premises is located and if the buyer completes the purchase, buyer will do so in material reliance on this Statement.

| _____ | _____ |
| Date | Tenant |

| _____ | _____ |
| By | Title |

Market Rent Survey*

	Subject		Area Competitors								
Address of property											
Location rating											
Age											
Percentage of occupancy											
Overall condition and appeal											
Amount of security deposit											
Minimum length of lease											
Children allowed											
Pets allowed											
Unit rents:	Rate	Per Sq Ft	Rate	Per Sq Ft	Rate	Per Sq Ft	Rate	Per Sq Ft	Rate	Per Sq Ft	Rate	Per Sq Ft
Efficiency											
One bedroom											
Two bedroom											
Appliances											
Furnished											
Unfurnished											
Utilities included											
Parking											

*Copyright © 2006 by Walter Sanford. To customize this document, download to your hard drive from www.waltersanford.com/insiderinvestingforms. The document can then be opened, edited, and printed using Microsoft Word or another popular word processing application.

(continued)

	Subject	Area Competitors			
Recreational Facilities:					
Clubhouse					
Pool					
Tennis courts					
Sauna					
Exercise facilities					
Other inclusions					

CHAPTER 14

Insider Questions That Will Help You Make Money

As you are doing the due diligence as only an insider can, you will meet people who will allow you to—for lack of a better phrase—"pick their brains." Many times, your position as a top real estate agent allows you access to the inner circle of decision makers—people like bank presidents, city planners, city officials, and appraisers. As you build your relationships with these people in pursuing your day-to-day business and developing your personal investment program, you will find that they are a valuable source of information.

In my career as an investor, these inner circle decision makers have given me many leads. Whenever I was meeting with one of them, I made it a habit to ask the following questions:

- What do you see as being the next hottest area in our town?
- Where is the smart money going right now?
- Do you know any areas that are receiving more interest than others as land acquisitions?
- What do you think of a purchase that I am contemplating at [address]?

If I am talking to a city planner, I ask the following questions:

- Do you know about any great deals that will be coming up for sale in our city?
- What are the needs of the city?
- What types of project would the city really get behind?
- Have any areas been rezoned recently for higher density, but the changes are not well known?
- What is the city's highest priority for new development or refurbishment?
- What land plays do you see going on right now?

If you are an insider and can talk to the people in your city who make decisions, you can find out what they know about future real estate investments as well as the one you are considering now.

I have successfully put together small groups of like-minded investors who meet for breakfast at least once a week. These people may be aware of transactions that they cannot pursue but that might be available to me, and they may know about trends that I might have missed. I have always trusted these masterminds to help me evaluate whether I should close. My greatest insider asset may be the brain trust around me!

It is important to ask questions of everyone involved in the real estate game because trends and opportunities can become clearer to you, pointing you in the right direction for purchases. Sometimes you do your best due diligence before you ever find the property.

CHAPTER 15

Insider Closing Strategies

Now you have made sure this property meets your investment criteria, cleared the contingencies, and negotiated the best possible price and concessions within a win-win framework. You have obtained financing and are awaiting the close of the property.

This is when you need to dot your i's, cross your t's, and make certain that everything you negotiated will come to fruition. Making a checklist will help you track all the players in the game and all the activities that you must complete prior to the close. As an insider, I know how important it is to attend to details.

Form 15.1 shows the closing checklist that I use both for my own purchases and the purchases of my clients. You will find it useful, because consistency of satisfactory service is one of the highest rated consumer values. This checklist is also valuable because it allows me to verify that every important item in the transaction has been completed and that I am leveraging additional business for my brokerage from insider investment dealings.

Closing pieces of real estate generally involves the same procedures. Since some items are consistently included, it is easy to confirm each one. Checklists force us to focus on what is important rather than on what may seem to be urgent, because minor urgent items can sometimes divert your actions from what is profitable and what makes clients happy.

Items That Require Attention before Closing

Constant fires seem to materialize in the closing process. I made a list of all the reasons that had delayed or prevented a closing in my 30 years of real estate transactions. This list was so lengthy that it became a major part of my listing presentations, FSBO presentations, and proof of commission value. I called it my "Closing Problems Checklist" and sent it to my clients so they could see the amount of work involved in closing a transaction. Giving this checklist to the other party when I was a principal in the transaction proved that I was trying to prepare for all the problems that could happen. It always made the buyer or seller on the other side appreciate that there was an insider on the opposite side.

There are many items that require attention prior to close. The two most frustrating items are insurance and the acquisition of an accurate appraisal (especially in a hot market).

The insurance pain can be cured by starting early. Many properties are not insurable by traditional insurance companies, so you must have some sort of government intervention by way of a risk pool. Your insurance agent will explain this to you, however, it is important to start early because the acquisition of insurance on a tough building will take time. Insurance must be started early in the closing process. Your insider status should carry some weight when the need for service comes up.

Because appraisals are an inexact science, they should be started early. As an insider, you have advantages. You can show up at the appraisal with comparables that support the value of the property. Not only will your clients appreciate this extra service, but as an insider, you can help the appraiser obtain the evaluation that achieves your goal of closing. It always made me nervous if the appraiser was not knowledgeable about the area or the values of comparable properties. If I suspected a problem, I immediately implemented my appraisal checklist to make sure that I (or my clients) received every benefit of the doubt. I also took the following six precautions:

1. I contacted the appraiser prior to the appraisal appointment to discuss relevant items about the property and what made the property more valuable than some of the comparables.

2. I made copies of all relevant comparables available to the appraiser by way of e-mail, fax, or hard copies—whatever the person preferred.

3. I contacted the sellers or the agent who represented the sellers to make certain that they had the property ready for showing in the best light.

4. I discussed with the property owners, or the agent representing them, the best times to avoid negative factors such as heavy traffic, low-flying airplanes, or rowdy neighbors when showing the property.

5. On difficult appraisals, I would meet with the appraiser on the site. Although I did this infrequently, sometimes it was necessary to make certain that the appraiser was seeing the property in the same light that I perceived it.

6. I would contact the appraiser for the results before the appraisal was submitted to the bank. If the appraisal was too low, I would look for any calculations or information that might help the appraiser bring the appraisal up to the required amount.

I am not suggesting that you should pad the file for the appraisal; however, keep in mind that if you have ready, willing, and able sellers or if *you* are the ready and able seller, the only thing separating them or you from a sale is the appraisal.

Another roadblock that might hinder a closing is the inspection report for the property. As you well know, inspectors come in all shapes and sizes—some qualified, some not as qualified. One of the largest challenges of closing may be an inspector relative—the father-in-law, brother-in-law, friend, or associate who has a reputation for being knowledgeable about the building trades. This person is drafted as an inexpensive alternative to hiring a professional. These pseudoinspectors will find every potential red flag, real or perceived, to guarantee that they have a statue in the inspector hall of fame. Their anxiety level about overlooking problems is intense because of the potential feedback of a family, friend, or associate. These hyperconscientious, sometimes dramatic, inspectors can be the kiss of death if you are representing the seller to a buyer or if you are selling one of your own properties.

Sometimes there is no easy alternative to amateur home inspectors because your buyers have requested them. However, it is prudent for you to interview any potential inspector to find out the person's qualifications and intentions. An inspector who is positive and cooperative about the purchase may be okay. However, if this person is rearing a six-gun and is ready for a shootout, you may want to take your buyer aside and suggest a professional home inspector in addition to or instead of the friend or relative.

Where I felt that the amateur home inspector would be the kiss of death—I contributed a portion of the cost for a professional home inspection. It is always smart to say to your buyer:

> *Mr. and Mrs. [name], the professional home inspector has a reputation to uphold in the community and will be held at a much higher level of responsibility regarding the inspection. On top of that, he is used to inspecting properties in this area, and he might have many appropriate suggestions for solving problems that he has seen in other properties with similar situations. May I suggest a local home inspector who has been certified through the American Society of Home Inspectors (ASHI)? This home inspector certification is recognized by professionals all over the country.*

This offer almost always allowed me to obtain a local nonbiased home inspector. Furthermore, the suggestions of the friend or relative would then be discounted and the inspector's opinions would receive greater respect. The negotiations will proceed more smoothly with a licensed professional behind the report.

Sending the cover letter shown in Form 15.2 and the Closing Problems Checklist (Form 15.3) to your client and to the other party with whom you are negotiating is an insider action that has two benefits:

1. If none of the items on the checklist happen, you will be looked on as the professional who prevented these things from happening.

2. If they do happen, the parties can at least say that they have been warned.

More Insider Closing Strategies

The previously mentioned letter and form will make everyone involved with the transaction aware of any potential problems. Implementing systems, working with a well-motivated buyer and seller, and having a well-written contract will prevent most problems. Distributing your Closing Problems Checklist to your buyers and sellers increases their perception of your value immensely and will help you expand your business from referrals. Your understanding of potential problems will put your clients on notice and you will be a hero!

The people who first notice and see problems are sometimes your team members. Your lender, closing professional, termite person, home warranty/home inspector, accountant, or attorney can be an early warning device on any of these items, and all of your team members should be appropriately counseled on how to cure problems quickly without involving too much of your time. Always use your insider advantage.

In California, we had escrows and escrow instructions. These escrow instructions are prepared after the purchase contract has been written, and they need to be signed. Early in my career, an escrow officer called me to let me know that the escrow instructions had not been signed. My question was, "Why didn't you call my clients and ask why the form was not signed?" The escrow officer was amazed that I would ask this, and she said, "Because they are your clients." My response—"Yes, and I am your client, so please handle it!" I am surprised that many real estate agents will jump when asked to perform a task for one of their affiliates. Your affiliates work with you and need to put out the fires that occur in their area of expertise. I have always been extremely loyal to my affiliates, but I do not like for them to delegate duties that should or could be theirs. It is their responsibility to put out as many fires as their authority permits. When they have a fire that only I can put out, then they should notify me. If you give your affiliates all your business and are totally loyal, they should be happy to perform a higher level of service, thus allowing you to accomplish the tasks that are really necessary to close your insider deal.

The next item of concern is inspection timing. There are four possible inspections:

1. My initial inspection. I do this when I am making the decision to purchase the property.

2. My postcontract inspection. This takes place after the contract has been accepted to determine that all items are in good working order.

3. The professional inspection by a certified home inspector or friend/associate/contractor. I generally do this at the same time as inspection number 2.

4. The final walk-through prior to close. This is to ensure that no damage has occurred during the closing process and that all negotiated repairs have been made.

All of these closings should be handled differently, and I deviate from the norm in many of these areas. The following paragraphs describe the most efficient and problem-free methods of handling inspections as an insider.

The first inspection should be done with as much care as possible or as time permits. If you are extremely interested in the property, it is prudent to list as many of the deficiencies in the contract as possible. This will prevent the seller from believing that you are a nibbler after the contract has been accepted. It is an up-front and proper negotiating technique to name easily, identifiable deficiencies and discuss how those deficiencies may affect the price or how they should be fixed. This inspection process usually takes care of most problems during negotiations.

You and the professional inspector make the second and third inspections after contract. The danger is deciding where to draw the line between real deficiency and negotiating for excusable repairs. Mention as many of the deficiencies as possible in the first inspection rather than in the second one. During the second inspection, the sellers have already decided that they have a sold piece of property and that the buyer is experiencing buyer's remorse. An inspection that comes back with new and unidentified problems is always laden with an excruciating negotiation process. Although fairness should always be at the forefront in these negotiations, this is not always a reality; please understand, there are no perfect properties. From the seller's standpoint, as many potential problems as possible should be mentioned in the contract, instead of after the inspection. Make sure that the buyer understands the difference between cosmetic changes and deficiencies.

The fourth or final inspection can be one of the most gut-wrenching experiences of the entire purchase or sale. Some buyers perceive this inspection as a treasure hunt. They suspect that the sellers are already boxing up belongings, have called the moving truck, and are ready to close. In fact, sometimes they have already made a deposit on a new property. This situation, right or wrong, puts the buyer in the position of having the most power and does not go unnoticed by most buyers. Be careful to emphasize that the final walk-through is not a treasure hunt. I do this by formalizing it in the contract. This is what I put in all contracts, whether I am the buyer or the seller:

Final walk-through is to be for the sole purpose of determining that the property is in the same condition as it was during the last inspection dated _____ , and that all requested repairs from the last inspection of _____ have been satis-factorily completed. No additional repairs can be requested if these were items that were discernible at the inspection date of _____ . The only repairs that can be requested at the final walk-through are repairs that were not made or improperly made from the inspection of _____ and/or items that have occurred that qualify as problems since the inspection of _____ .

This allows me to let everyone know that the only way that they can nibble at the end is if repairs already requested were improperly done or there was new damage to the property. There will be no treasure hunt moments before the close.

Just because you are an insider, do not get lazy! A seller may be tempted to strip a property of any valuable items, to neglect necessary maintenance, or fail to do a thorough cleaning job in the last days of ownership. Since you will never be in a better position to demand compliance than when your pen is poised over the check for the purchase price, make sure you inspect the property thoroughly just before you complete the transaction. Insist on correction of any violations of the agreement of sale. Take a copy of the agreement of sale and this book with you. You should also take an instant camera or digital camera and a witness.

Don't be timid. Turn on the heating system, even if it is August. Check to see that everything that is supposed to be in good working order *is* working. Look for damage that may have occurred since you initially inspected the property.

Check to see if the owner has stripped the building. Are the drapes, refrigerator, light fixtures, and plants the same ones you bargained for?

Have tenants who were supposed to be out by settlement departed, or are they still moving and creating a mess as they go? If so, demand that the settlement be postponed or the proceeds due seller be held in escrow until the buyer gives written permission to disburse.

Is the property in the condition agreed to? "Broom clean" is the phrase commonly used. If it looks like a shovel-wielding crew of eight will be necessary to clean the place, demand a postponement. You have been walking on eggshells because of your insider status, you have a superior knowledge, a license, and you don't want a bad reputation for taking an unfair advantage, but do not confuse that with being stupid by allowing a seller to walk all over you.

Settlements are a "speak now or forever hold your peace" event. Theoretically, you can sue after settlement, but in practice, such suits are rarely worth the effort they require. Your ability to refuse to go through with settlement is your best guarantee of fair treatment. Lawsuits hurt your reputation!

You should have the advice of your attorney before refusing to complete settlement. The seller has the right to sue you for specific performance or for damages if you fail to live up to the terms of the agreement. The legal cure is generally worse than the disease, so a wise seller should comply with your fair demands.

Form 15.4 is a checklist of items to take to your closing. The settlement, or closing, is the final phase of your investment acquisition. By this time, you have established prudent investment criteria, searched the area thoroughly to find a property that meets your criteria, and negotiated to get the best possible terms. Your main task at settlement is to make sure you are getting exactly what you bargained for and exactly what you are about to pay for.

Downloadable FORM 15.1
Closing Checklist*

Address of Sold Property: _____ Price: _____

MLS#: _____ Projected Closing Date: _____

Sellers	**Buyers**

Name: _____

Address: _____

Forwarding Address: _____

Phone H: _____

W: _____

W: _____

Pager: _____

Cellular: _____

E-mail: _____

Phone H: _____

W: _____

W: _____

Pager: _____

Cellular: _____

E-mail: _____

*Copyright © 2006 by Walter Sanford. To customize this document, download to your hard drive from www.waltersanford .com/insiderinvestingforms. The document can then be opened, edited, and printed using Microsoft Word or another popular word processing application.

Coop Agent

Name: _____

Firm: _____

Address: _____

Phone: W: _____ H: _____

Fax: _____ Cellular: _____

Pager: _____ E-mail: _____

Closing

Name of Officer: _____

Company: _____

Address: _____

Phone: _____

Fax: _____ E-mail: _____

Escrow No.: _____ Date of Opening: _____

Contingency Closing

Name of Officer: _____

Company: _____

Address: _____

Phone: _____

Fax: _____ E-mail: _____

Escrow No.: _____ Date of Opening: _____

(continued)

Contingency Closing

Name of Officer: _____

Company: _____

Address: _____

Phone: _____

Fax: _____ E-mail: _____

Escrow No.: _____ Date of Opening: _____

Lender

Name of Firm: _____

Agent: _____ Broker: _____

Address: _____

Loan No.: _____

Phone W: _____ H: _____

Fax: _____ Pager: _____

Cellular: _____ E-mail: _____

Second Lender

Name of Firm: _____

Agent: _____ Broker: _____

Address: _____

Loan No.: _____

Phone W: _____ H: _____

Fax: _____ Pager: _____

Cellular: _____ E-mail: _____

Title Insurance

Name of Firm: _____

Rep: _____

Called in: _____

Phone W: _____ H: _____

Fax: _____ Pager: _____

Cellular: _____ E-mail: _____

Short Rate: _____ Binder: _____

      (Notify Title Rep)

Name of Firm: _____

Rep: _____

Called in: _____

Phone W: _____ H: _____

Fax: _____ Pager: _____

Cellular: _____ E-mail: _____

Notes: _____

_____

_____

_____

Financing:	Commission:
Deposit _____	Gross _____
Add'l Deposit _____	Concessions _____
Balance Down _____	Referral Fee _____
1st _____	Net Commissions _____
2nd _____	Note Amount _____
3rd _____	Terms _____
Total Sales Price _____	Net Cash _____

(continued)

Checklist to Close

1. Deposit Receipt: To Client: _____   Recv'd from Client: _____   File: _____

2. Counter Offers: To Client: _____   Recv'd from Client: _____   File: _____

   Counter to Counter: To Client: _____   Recv'd from Client: _____   File: _____

3. Escrow Instructions: File

4. Home Protection Plan:

   Company:_____

   Ordered: _____   Phone: _____

   Confirmation: _____   Rep: _____

5. Property Inspection: Name: _____

   Address: _____

   Ordered: _____   Appointment: _____   Report on File: _____

   Repairs Agreed: _____   Repairs Done: _____

6. Permits: In file: _____

7. In Escrow Letter: Receipted to Agent: _____

   Outside Affiliates: _____   _____   _____

8. Seller Carry Back Disclosure:

   Buyer: Sent: _____   Received: _____

   Seller: Sent: _____   Received: _____

   Agent: Sent: _____   Received: _____

9. FIRPTA: Received from Seller: _____

   Received from Agent: _____

   File: _____   To Agent: _____

10. Listing Disclosure:

    To Buyer: _____   Received: _____

    To Seller: _____   Received: _____

    To Agent: _____   Received: _____

11. Agency Disclosure and Confirmation:

    To Buyer: _____   Received: _____

    To Seller: _____   Received: _____

    To Agent: _____   Received: _____

12. Environmental Hazards Booklet:

    To Buyer: _____   Received: _____

    To Seller: _____   Received: _____

    To Agent: _____   Received: _____

13. Earthquake Safety Booklet:

    To Buyer: _____   Received: _____

    To Seller: _____   Received: _____

    To Agent: _____   Received: _____

14. Sale Pending Rider Up: _____

15. Caddy Tray/Brochure/Lockbox Picked Up (If Applicable): _____

16. Homeowners' Documents: Receipt to Agent: _____

17. Move Card: _____

18. Sale Board: _____

19. Cash Flow Sheet: _____

20. Termite:

    Other: _____

    Limit: _____

    Ordered Inspection: _____   Date of Work: _____

    Sellers Notified: _____   Sellers Notified: _____

21. Garage Inspection:

    Date Ordered: _____   N/A: _____

(continued)

Downloadable FORM 15.1   *(Continued)*

22. Appraiser: _____

    Name and Address: _____

    Works for Whom? _____ Appoint for: _____

    Seller Notified: _____ Time: _____

    Who to meet Appraiser: _____

    Comps Needed: Yes   No

        Parameters Needed: _____

        2nd Appraiser: _____

        Works for Whom? _____ Appoint for: _____

        Seller Notified: _____ Time: _____

        Who to meet Appraiser: _____

23. Loan approval: _____ By Whom: _____ Date: _____

    Conditions: _____

24. Order Termite Completion: _____

25. Call sign down/get riders/lockbox/caddy tray: _____

At Close of Escrow

1. Report Sold to MLS: _____

2. Take out of up books: _____

3. Thank You letters:

    Client 1: _____

    Client 2: _____

    Client 3: _____

    Other Broker: _____

    Lender: _____

    Other: _____

4. Just Sold Cards (Notify Mail House): _____

5. Print in Anniversary database: _____

6. Take off all web sites mentioned in listing checklist: _____

7. Sales to Date Ledger: _____

8. Database/Red Dot/Have/Want (both sides of transaction): _____

9. Send sold info to Press Telegram "Real Estate Desk": _____

10. Closing Statement and Letter dated January 10th in file: _____

11. Make Walter ask for Referral: _____

12. E & O Insurance Transaction Log: _____

13. Closing statement, and copy of check in file: _____

14. Walter's office questionnaire sent to client: _____

15. Request for moving mailer card addressed phone numbers: _____

16. Moving card mailed: _____

17. This file cannot close without Testimonial Letter or explanation of challenge

to negotiate: _____

18. Referral Fee Payments: _____

19. Call all referrals of move card: _____

20. Send referral/finder's fee:

    Name: _____

    Phone W: _____ H: _____

    Cellular: _____ Pager: _____

    Fax: _____ E-mail: _____

    Amount $_____ Date Sent: _____

Downloadable FORM 15.2
Cover Letter to Closing Problem Checklist*

Date

Name

Address

City, ST Zip

Name:

Congratulations are in order now that we have a deal! Please remember though, the real work is just beginning.

We have agreed on the purchase price, terms, and general conditions that have to be met to close the sale.

Let's try to remember that sometimes unexpected things happen and problems can creep up. If we work together, we will be able to overcome any challenge and close this transaction. I have enclosed a copy of my closing problem checklist so that you can maintain vigilance in identifying any potential challenges.

A few very important things to remember are the following:

1. Whenever any paperwork is needed, signatures are required, or additional information is requested, please facilitate this as quickly as possible.

2. Please keep our primary objectives in sight at all times. Let's focus on resolving challenges, and keep our lines of communication open at all times!

3. Finally, I am here for you. I want this transaction to flow as smoothly as possible for you, so please feel free to ask me questions at any time.

Thank you and again, congratulations!

Sincerely,

Walter Sanford

Sanford Systems

*Copyright © 2006 by Walter Sanford. To customize this document, download to your hard drive from www.waltersanford .com/insiderinvestingforms. The document can then be opened, edited, and printed using Microsoft Word or another popular word processing application.

Downloadable FORM 15.3
Closing Problem Checklist*

It is the wise client who prepares for problems before they happen! I also believe in this concept for my business. My closing problems checklist keeps me busy every day. Since no escrow is *closed* until it is **closed**, the following items are our potential roadblocks.

Years of experience and successful closings have armed me with the tools to overcome each and every problem encountered here; however, it would be unfair for me to say that every problem can be solved. I have placed a delay of closing estimate next to each problem and the ones with daggers (†) are potential deal killers:

Lender	**Delay**
1. Lender does not properly prequalify borrower.	2 weeks or [†]
2. Lender decides to disapprove borrower at last minute.	2 weeks or [†]
3. Lender decides against property at last minute.	2 weeks or [†]
4. Lender wants property repaired or cleaned prior to close.	1 to 3 weeks
5. Lender raises rates, points, or costs.	2 weeks or [†]
6. Borrower does not qualify because of a late addition of information.	2 weeks or [†]
7. Lender requires, last minute, a reappraisal.	2 weeks or [†]
8. The borrower does not like the fine print in the loan documents that we receive 3 days before close.	3 days or [†]
9. Lender loses file.	1 to 3 weeks
10. The lender does not simultaneously ask for information from the buyer, loan officer asks for information in bits and pieces.	1 to 4 weeks

*Copyright © 2006 by Walter Sanford. To customize this document, download to your hard drive from www.waltersanford.com/insiderinvestingforms. The document can then be opened, edited, and printed using Microsoft Word or another popular word processing application.

(continued)

The Cooperative Agent	**Delay**
1. Won't return phone calls.	1 to 3 weeks
2. Transfers to another office.	1 week
3. Did not prequalify the client for motivation.	2 weeks or [†]
4. Goes on vacation and leaves no one to handle file.	1 to 4 weeks
5. Does not understand or lacks experience in real estate.	1 week or [†]
6. Poor people skills with buyer.	1 to 3 weeks
7. Gets client upset over minor points.	1 to 3 weeks
8. Does not communicate with client.	1 to 4 weeks

The Buyer	**Delay**
1. Did not tell the truth on loan application.	1 week or [†]
2. Did not tell the truth to the agent.	1 week or [†]
3. Submits incorrect tax returns to lender.	4 weeks or [†]
4. Lacks motivation.	1 week or [†]
5. Source of down payment changes.	1 week or [†]
6. Family members do not like purchase.	1 week or [†]
7. Is too picky regarding condition.	1 week or [†]
8. Finds another property that is a better deal.	1 week or [†]

9. They are "nibblers" (always negotiating).   1 week or [†]

10. The buyers bring an attorney into the picture.   2 weeks or [†]

11. They do not execute paperwork in a timely manner.   3 weeks or [†]

12. They do not deliver their money in a "check cleared"
    fashion to the closing agent.   1 to 2 weeks

13. Job change, illness, divorce, or other financial.
    setback.   3 weeks or [†]

14. Comes up short on money.   1 week or [†]

15. Does not obtain insurance in a timely manner.   1 to 4 weeks

Escrow   ### Delay

1. Fails to notify agents of unsigned or unreturned
    documents so that the agents can cure the problems
    relating to same.   1 week or [†]

2. Fails to obtain information from beneficiaries,
    lien holders, title companies, insurance companies, or
    lenders in a timely manner.   1 week or [†]

3. Lets principals leave town without getting all
    necessary signatures.   1 to 2 weeks

4. Incorrect at interpreting or assuming aspects of the
    transaction and then passing these items on to related
    parties such as lenders, attorneys, buyers, or sellers.   1 week or [†]

5. Too busy.   1 to 3 weeks

6. Loses paperwork.   1 to 3 weeks

7. Incorrectly prepares paperwork.   1 to 3 weeks

(continued)

8.	Does not pass on valuable information fast enough.	1 to 4 weeks
9.	Does not coordinate well so that many items can be done simultaneously.	1 to 4 weeks

Seller   Delay

1.	Loses motivation (e.g., job transfer did not go through).	1 week or [†]
2.	Illness, divorce, etc.	1 week or [†]
3.	Has hidden defects that are subsequently discovered.	1 week or [†]
4.	Unknown defects are discovered.	1 week or [†]
5.	Home inspection reveals average amount of small defects that seller is unwilling-willing to repair.	1 week or [†]
6.	Gets an attorney involved.	1 week or [†]
7.	Removes property from the premises that the buyer believed was included.	1 to 3 weeks
8.	Is unable to clear up problems or liens.	1 week or [†]
9.	Last-minute solvable liens are discovered.	1 to 3 weeks
10.	Seller did not own 100% of property as previously disclosed.	1 week or
11.	Seller thought partners signatures were "no problem" but they were.	1 week or [†]
12.	Seller leaves town without giving anyone power of attorney.	1 to 4 weeks

13. The notary did not make a clear stamp. when notarizing the seller's signatures.   3 days to 1 week

14. Seller delays the projected move-out date.   1 day or †

Acts of God	**Delay**
1. Earthquake, tornado, fire, slides, etc.	1 week or †

The Appraisal	**Delay**
1. The appraiser is not local and misunderstands the market.	1 to 3 weeks
2. No comparable sales available.	1 week or †
3. Appraiser delays (too busy, etc.).	1 to 3 weeks
4. Incorrect appraisal.	1 to 3 weeks
5. Appraisal too low.	1 week or †

Inspection Company	**Delay**
1. Too picky.	1 day or †
2. Scares buyer.	1 week or †
3. Infuriates seller.	1 week or †
4. Makes mistakes.	1 to 3 weeks
5. Delays report.	1 week or †

(continued)

133

Title Company	Delay
1. Does not find liens or problems until last minute.	1 week or [†]
2. Does not bend rules on small problems.	1 to 3 weeks
3. Poor service.	1 to 3 weeks
4. Loses paperwork.	1 to 2 weeks

The limited time between contract acceptance and close always poses a challenge. I want you to understand these potential problems for the following reasons:

1. A transaction cannot close until escrow has cleared up any and all of the previously mentioned problems.

2. To let you know that I have great experience in heading off these potential pitfalls.

3. To make these pitfalls clear to all the parties that we are working with so that problems can be discovered early.

4. To make you aware of these pitfalls so that you can warn me of any potential problems.

Once again, congratulations!

Sincerely,

Walter Sanford
Sanford Systems

Downloadable FORM 15.4
Items to Take to Your Closing*

Be sure to take the following with you:

_____ Pen and paper

_____ Copy of the agreement of sale

_____ List of the mortgage terms you bargained for

_____ List of the deed terms you bargained for

_____ Your estimate of the amount of additional cash (above your deposit) you will need to complete settlement

_____ A certified check for the amount (cleared funds)

_____ All written estimates of fees to be charged

_____ Any documents requested by the lender or seller, such as the fire insurance policy and a receipt for the premium

_____ The rent schedule and deposit schedule

_____ Notarized documents signed by person who could not attend settlement

_____ Receipts for any fees paid prior to settlement

_____ A copy of the assumed deed of trust or mortgage

_____ A copy of the assumed note

_____ An explanation of all of the charges to the buyer and seller (settlement statement)

_____ A receipt for all payments you have made for whatever purpose

_____ A bill of sale for any personal property you have purchased separately from the real estate

_____ The commission check, if you have a real estate license and are participating in the commission or if you are signing it over toward your down payment

_____ Termite certification

_____ Title insurance policy

_____ Fire insurance policy

_____ Liability insurance policy

_____ Mortgage insurance policy, if any

_____ Survey

*Copyright © 2006 by Walter Sanford. To customize this document, download to your hard drive from www.waltersanford .com/insiderinvestingforms. The document can then be opened, edited, and printed using Microsoft Word or another popular word processing application.

(continued)

_____ Prorated rents for the remainder of the rent period

_____ Security deposits and interest, if local law requires payment of interest

_____ Any repair money agreed on

_____ Any apartment building licenses in effect

_____ All leases on the property

_____ A statement of the amount of your mortgage payment and payment book

_____ Certificate of occupancy

_____ Estoppel certificates

_____ Inventory of the amount of fuel in the tank, if oil is used

_____ Sign permits, if any

_____ Letter to tenants signed by seller stating that the property has been sold to you and that rents are to be paid to you henceforth

_____ Copies of warranties and instruction manuals for building equipment

_____ Credit reports and other records on tenants

_____ Keys to every door in the building

CHAPTER 16

Setting Up Your Insider Ownership Paperwork

Congratulations! Through your insider efforts, you have obtained a great building for yourself. At this point, you must decide where your ownership is going to take you. Figure 16.1 shows a simple flowchart that can explain your options.

You have a lot of opportunities. Whereas most investment programs talk about acquiring property and either refinancing it to buy more or selling it to gain a property, or possibly even exchanging it, my passion—and the point of this book—has been to hold the property. I maximize the commission I earn from my real estate business, use that money as a down payment for acquiring insider opportunities, and then I own properties that produce cash flow. I use that cash flow to improve them and pay off mortgages as time goes on.

As discussed, I am assuming that you are a great real estate agent, and that with your insider advantages, you can provide your down payments from your business. Taking advantage of the acquisition hold-and-improve strategy increases your net cash flow every year and allows the magic of appreciation, equity paydown, and cash flow to develop a free-and-clear property prior to your retirement.

Now is the time to decide what you are going to do. If you choose the refinance equation, you could be acquiring more debt on the property than the property can handle, preventing yourself from weathering any tough times in the real estate market. If you sell the property, you cannot take advantage of the magic of cash flow, equity paydown, and appreciation. You will be subject to the cost of sale and also the amount the IRS imposes on you. If you choose the exchange method, you may get into bigger and better properties, and I certainly do endorse that; however, there are always the costs of an exchange. It is time to make the decision about your goals for this property. Think about what you really want.

FIGURE 16.1   The Real Estate Decision Tree

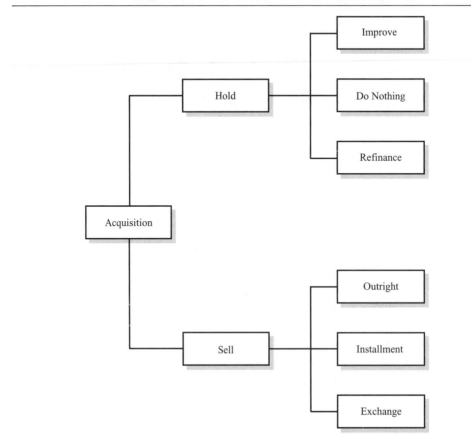

Insider Ownership Paperwork

At this point, you should start putting together your Property Summary Folder, which is where you will keep all the information about your real estate investment. My folders include a photo of the property and the items listed in Form 16.1.

The property summary gives you a shorthand view of the costs of buying your successful piece of real estate. I put all this information into a folder that is divided into three sections. On the left-hand side of Section One, I put Form 16.1, along with all the documents that were necessary to purchase the property: the original deposit receipts, the escrow instructions, inspection reports, and all other negotiations that went on during the purchase of the property. On the right-hand side of the first section, I put all loan documents, trust deeds, and promissory notes. If I were refinancing the property, I would put those documents on the top.

In Section Two of the folder on the left-hand side, I put all printed applications and rental agreements. I also put all advertising done on the property including flyers. On the right-hand side, I insert Form 16.2, which has all the information for repairs and capital expenses spent on the property. I also place insurance information (Form 16.3) in this section.

On the left-hand side of Section Three, I place my investment analysis showing my investment return for the piece of real estate. This changes as my income goes up, so I do this once a year for my properties. Forms 16.4 through 16.8 are used to determine investment return. Form 16.9 is a worksheet to calculate the replacement reserve needed to maintain a property.

Completing Your Property Summary Folder

As an insider, I am well aware of how necessary it is for owners to keep a detailed file on investments. In the previous section (Section Three) of my file, on the right-hand side, I keep all documents that I might need if I were ever to sell the property—which, of course, I try not to do!

We are now ready to manage our property and gain more insider benefits.

Downloadable FORM 16.1
Property Summary*

Photo

Goes

Here

*Copyright © 2006 by Walter Sanford. To customize this document, download to your hard drive from www.waltersanford .com/insiderinvestingforms. The document can then be opened, edited, and printed using Microsoft Word or another popular word processing application.

Downloadable FORM 16.1   *(Continued)*

Address: _____

City: _____ Zip: _____

Purchase Price: _____ Acquisition Date: _____

Allocation to Improvements: $_____

Closing Costs Not Expensed: $_____

Total Amount Subject to Cost Recovery: $_____

Type of Cost Recovery Used: $_____

Adjusted Basis Schedule: $_____

Property is being held in what name: _____

Date Purchased—Offer: _____ Closing: _____

Briefly state terms of original offer: _____

_____

_____

State changes made and if pertinent, state the reasons: _____

_____

_____

Final Terms: _____

_____

Reasons for purchasing this property: _____

_____

Are any other people (or corporations) involved? State terms: _____

_____

Financing Information: Purchase Price: _____

Down Payment: _____

Balance: _____

(continued)

Balance to be paid as follows:

Loan 1 (If It Exists)	Loan 2 (If It Exists)	Loan 3 (If It Exists)
Payee	Payee	Payee
Loan #	Loan #	Loan #
Amount	Amount	Amount
Monthly payment	Monthly payment	Monthly payment
Interest rate	Interest rate	Interest rate
Special terms	Special terms	Special terms
Recording numbers	Recording numbers	Recording numbers

Property Summary

Loan 1   Loan 2   Loan 3

If more information on any of these loans needs mentioning, check box and write on back, "Seller's Equity to be paid in" the following way:

Amount of equity (note): _____ Document used: _____

Is a copy of the note and legal instrument in this file?   Yes   No

If not, where is it kept (or recorded)? _____

Are all loans being assumed?   Yes   No

If not, please write details of the terms on the back.

List here all the documents for purchasing this property that are included in this file:

1. _____

2. _____

3. _____

4. _____

5. _____

6. _____

Closing costs (attach closing statement): _____

_____

Instructions for executors in case of death or disability: _____

_____

_____

_____

_____

_____

_____

Downloadable FORM 16.2
Insurance/Fix-Up*

Policy No.: _____   Agent's Phone No.: _____

Coverage: Building: _____   Contents: _____

    Liability: _____   Appurtenant Structures: _____

    Other: _____

Is this policy being taken over from previous owner?   Yes   No

If yes, are the proper documents executed and available for transferring the policy and any funds held in escrow? Explain: _____

_____

_____

_____

_____

Other Information on Capital Improvements:

      Ck #_____ For _____ Amt _____

      Ck #_____ For _____ Amt _____

      Ck #_____ For _____ Amt _____

      Ck #_____ For _____ Amt _____

      Ck #_____ For _____ Amt _____

      Ck #_____ For _____ Amt _____

      Ck #_____ For _____ Amt _____

      Ck #_____ For _____ Amt _____

      Ck #_____ For _____ Amt _____

      Ck #_____ For _____ Amt _____

      Ck #_____ For _____ Amt _____

      Ck #_____ For _____ Amt _____

*Copyright © 2006 by Walter Sanford. To customize this document, download to your hard drive from www.waltersanford .com/insiderinvestingforms. The document can then be opened, edited, and printed using Microsoft Word or another popular word processing application.

Downloadable FORM 16.2 *(Continued)*

Ck #_____ For _____ Amt _____

Ck #_____ For _____ Amt _____

Ck #_____ For _____ Amt _____

Ck #_____ For _____ Amt _____

Ck #_____ For _____ Amt _____

Ck #_____ For _____ Amt _____

Ck #_____ For _____ Amt _____

Ck #_____ For _____ Amt _____

Ck #_____ For _____ Amt _____

Ck #_____ For _____ Amt _____

Ck #_____ For _____ Amt _____

Ck #_____ For _____ Amt _____

Ck #_____ For _____ Amt _____

Ck #_____ For _____ Amt _____

Ck #_____ For _____ Amt _____

If more lines are needed, add another sheet or write on back.
Check here if additional lines are used. ❏

Information on Capital Improvements: _____

_____

_____

_____

_____

_____

_____

_____

_____

_____

Downloadable FORM 16.3

Insurance Coverage Summary*

Property: _____ Date: _____

Address: _____ Owner: _____

Kind of Coverage	Insured by (Company)	Agent: Name/Phone	Amount of Coverage	Period		Annual Premium
				From	To	
Fire and extended coverage						
Liability						
Boiler						
Workmen's compensation						
Rent income						
Employee fidelity bond						
Money and securities						
Plate glass						
Burglary and theft						
Vandalism						
Automobile: collision, bodily injury, property damage						

*Copyright © 2006 by Walter Sanford. To customize this document, download to your hard drive from www.waltersanford.com/insiderinvestingforms. The document can then be opened, edited, and printed using Microsoft Word or another popular word processing application.

Downloadable FORM 16.4
Residential Investment Analysis Property and Investor Data Summary*

Property Address: _____ Investor: _____

Prepared by: _____ Date: _____

A. Purchase Data

Purchase Price   (a) $_____

Allocation: Land _____%   Improvement _____%

Land Value $ _____

Improvement Value (b) $_____

B. Financing

	Amount	Rate	Annual Interest
1st Loan	$_____	X _____%	= $_____
2nd Loan	$_____	X _____%	= $_____
Totals	(c) $_____		(d) $_____
Down Payment	$_____		
Plus: Closing Costs +	$_____		
Initial Investment	(e) $_____		

C. Operating Data

Gross Scheduled Income

(Monthly Rent $_____ X 12) = (f) $_____

Annual Vacancy Allowance (_____%)   (g) $_____

Annual Operating Expenses:

Property Taxes	$_____
Insurance	$_____
Utilities	$_____
Maintenance	$_____
Other	$_____
Total Operating Expense	(h) $_____

*Copyright © 2006 by Walter Sanford. To customize this document, download to your hard drive from www.waltersanford .com/insiderinvestingforms. The document can then be opened, edited, and printed using Microsoft Word or another popular word processing application.

(continued)

D. Investment Data

(i)   Investor Tax Bracket _____%

(j)   Holding Period _____ Yrs.

(k)   Annual Property Appreciation Rate _____%

(l)   Projected Cost of Sale _____%

(m) Before Tax Investment Rate _____%

Downloadable FORM 16.5
Residential Investment Analysis Before-Tax Financing Analysis*

A. Gross Operating Income

Gross Scheduled Income (f) $_____

Less: Vacancy Allowance (g)   – $_____

Gross Operating Income $_____

B. Net Operating Income (NOI)

Gross Operating Income $_____

Less: Total Operating Expense (h)   – $_____

Net Operating Income $_____

C. Cash Flow Before Taxes (CFBT)

Net Operating Income $_____

Less: Annual Interest Payments (d)   – $_____

Cash Flow Before Taxes $_____

*Copyright © 2006 by Walter Sanford. To customize this document, download to your hard drive from www.waltersanford .com/insiderinvestingforms. The document can then be opened, edited, and printed using Microsoft Word or another popular word processing application.

Downloadable FORM 16.6
Residential Investment Analysis Annual Cash Flow after Taxes*

A. Taxable Income or (Loss)

Net Operating Income $_____

Less: Interest Payment (d)   – $_____

Less: Cost Recovery (Compute Below)

To Calculate Cost Recovery	
Improvement Value (b) $_____	
Divided By: Annual Cost Recovery $_____	– $_____

Taxable Income or (Loss) $_____

B. Tax Savings or Tax Liability

Taxable Income or (Loss) $_____

Times: (i) Tax Bracket   X _____%

Tax Savings (if negative)
     or
Tax Liability (if positive) $_____

C. Cash Flow After Taxes

Tax Savings
     or
Tax Liability $_____

Plus: Cash Flow Before Taxes

(From Form 16.5)   + $_____

Cash Flow After Taxes (CFAT) $_____

If Cash Flow Before Taxes is negative: A tax savings will reduce the negative cash flow. A tax liability will increase the negative cash flow.

If Cash Flow Before Taxes is positive: A tax savings will increase the positive cash flow. A tax liability will reduce the positive cash flow.

*Copyright © 2006 by Walter Sanford. To customize this document, download to your hard drive from www.waltersanford .com/insiderinvestingforms. The document can then be opened, edited, and printed using Microsoft Word or another popular word processing application.

Downloadable FORM 16.7

Residential Investment Analysis After-Tax Proceeds from Sale*

A. Projected Sales Price

Purchase Price(i) (n) a $_____ (PV)

[(k) _____ % appreciation for (j) _____ yrs.]

Projected Sales Price (Solve for) (FV) $_____

B. Taxable Gain on Home Sale

Projected Sales Price (PSP) $_____

Less: Sales Cost (l) _____% X PSP – $_____

Less: Adjusted Basis (Compute Below)

To Calculate Adjusted Basis

Purchase Price (a) $_____

Plus: Closing Cost @ Purchase + $_____

Less: Total Cost Recovery: – $_____

$_____ Annual Cost Recovery (Form 16.6)

(j) X _____ Holding Period – $_____

Adjusted Basis $_____

Taxable Gain on Sale

C. Tax Due from Sale

Taxable Gain or Sale $_____

Times: Maximum Tax Rate   X_____%

Maximum Possible Tax Due $_____

*Copyright © 2006 by Walter Sanford. To customize this document, download to your hard drive from www.waltersanford .com/insiderinvestingforms. The document can then be opened, edited, and printed using Microsoft Word or another popular word processing application.

(continued)

D. After-Tax Proceeds from Form Sale

Projected Sale Price	$ _____
Less: Sales Costs	– $ _____
Mortgage Balance Due (c)	– $ _____
Tax Due from Sale	– $ _____
After-Tax Proceeds from Sales	$ _____

Downloadable FORM 16.8
Residential Investment Analysis Performance Summary*

A. Initial Investment (e) $_____

B. Future Value of Cash Flows
   after Taxes (CFAT, From Form 16.6; PMT) $_____

Before Tax Investment Rate (m) _____ %

Investor Tax Bracket (i) _____ %

After Tax Rate (Form 16.6) (i) _____ %

Holding Period (j) _____ (n) _____ %

Amount Accumulated (Solve for FV) $_____

C. Wealth Positive After (j)_____ Years

Amount Accumulated $_____

Plus: After-Tax Proceeds from Sale (Form 16.7) + $_____

Wealth Position $_____

D. Yield Factor

Wealth Position (FV)

Initial Investment (e) (PV)

Holding Period (j) (N)

E. Percentage Earned Per Dollar Invested Each Year

Solve for (i) _____ %

Note: If CFAT is positive, the rate represents the after-tax yield that annual cash flows would earn if invested in a relatively safe and liquid type investment. If CFAT is negative, the rate represents the after-tax opportunity cost of using investment capital to meet the annual deficit.

*Copyright © 2006 by Walter Sanford. To customize this document, download to your hard drive from www.waltersanford.com/insiderinvestingforms. The document can then be opened, edited, and printed using Microsoft Word or another popular word processing application.

Downloadable FORM 16.9

Replacement Reserve Worksheet*

Property: _____

_____

Item	Remaining Replacement ÷ Useful Costs	Life	Annual Reserve ÷ 12 = Requirement	Monthly Reserve Requirement
Building				
Painting, Interior				
Painting, Exterior				
Roof				
Heating/AC Sys.				
Water Heater				

*Copyright © 2006 by Walter Sanford. To customize this document, download to your hard drive from www.waltersanford .com/insiderinvestingforms. The document can then be opened, edited, and printed using Microsoft Word or another popular word processing application.

Downloadable FORM 16.9 *(Continued)*

Carpet/Flooring				
Appliances				
Refrigerators				
Ranges				
Dishwashers				
Garbage Disposals				
Washers				
Dryers				

(continued)

Downloadable FORM 16.9   *(Continued)*

Grounds				
Fencing				
Landscaping				
Driveway/Parking				
Amenities				
Swimming Pool				
Tennis Court				
Recreation Room				

Downloadable FORM 16.9   *(Continued)*

Furnishings				
Total Reserve Requirement			$	$

Prepared by: _____ Approved by: _____

Date: _____ Date: _____

CHAPTER 17

Insider Tenant Acquisition

Y ou need to run your business like a business. You want to reap the benefits of your real estate investments and use your insider pull to attract more tenants. Here are some of the ways I use my insider advantage:

• I use the insider communication systems among all real estate agents that are supplied by my Board of Realtors®. I e-mail all my peers when a vacant unit becomes available for rental. Many real estate agents have clients who are one to a few years away from purchasing a property. People who have just sold are taking advantage of an overheated real estate market, pulling out the equity and renting while hoping for a possible repurchase toward the bottom of the real estate market. This has happened in swing states such as California and Florida, where the difference between top and bottom of the market has been as much as 40 percent. Taking the money off the table and renting has been a smart financial move for many. This especially is true under the new tax laws that allow you to take most, if not all, of your *winnings* tax free.

• Many times, while dealing with buyers and sellers, I identify people who would be perfect for my units. They might be clients or friends of a client who are not ready to commit to a piece of real estate. Sometimes they want to rent so that they can become familiar with the area before they buy a property.

• Many of my seller lead generation systems produce tenant leads, as do my buyer lead generation systems such as tenant-occupied listings. I solicit all tenant-occupied listings that are new on the market by contacting the tenants in the listing and letting them know that the house they live in is about to be sold. I discuss the advantages of home ownership and let them know that many times a mortgage can be more affordable than rent. If that does not fit their needs, these tenants still need a place to live, and I can offer them choices from my rental inventory.

• Occasionally, a transaction has "fires" that you just cannot put out. The seller may have committed to move, but their new property will not close on time and they need an emergency home to move into. Or you have a buyer whose chosen property becomes unavailable for one reason or another. They have already committed to move from their present home and now are in desperate need of temporary housing.

- Much of my business has come from relocation moves that I found out about through my relationships with local human resource departments. It was always a profitable service. As a trusted source of rental properties for executives moving into our city, I had a huge leg up on the competition. My reputation as the *total real estate resource* encouraged people to call me and helped me control the move in/move out of the personnel in major companies in my area.

- In my acquisition of professional mailing lists, such as the accounts of attorneys, I always stressed that I had rentals available for their clients' needs. Many times, attorneys appreciated my ability to move one party of a divorcing couple into a suitable rental property.

It can go the other way, too. In my insider management agreement (see Chapter 18), I ask for two-year leases. Many times, tenants would like to end the lease early. They can do that by keeping the lease payments current and paying all expenses of the property while I try to re-rent it. They can also buy a property utilizing my real estate brokerage services (or my wife's). If they buy a house through us and we earn a commission, they can walk from the lease. Being an insider allows many opportunities for profit.

Having rentals available in your real estate business not only will add to the value that you offer all your clients, but also will consistently find you a rich, new source of excellent tenants and many times, buyers, too.

CHAPTER 18

Magic Management by an Insider

Managing properties can be an absolute nightmare or a huge profit source depending on the documentation and systems that you implement. Many top real estate agents have a management division within their office. This division is usually started and grows by serving investor clients or by managing the properties that the real estate agent owns. Many top agents leave the business to start their own management companies. Form 18.1 is the agreement that I used for managing my investors' properties. Being an insider allows real estate agents to horizontally integrate their business. By using insider secrets to choose and manage investments, agents can cultivate another form of income. It is important to take management seriously, whether for yourself or for your clients. I have 14 *golden rules* of insider property management:

1. Attractive properties that trigger an emotional response will attract a higher caliber of tenants, rent faster, and can demand a higher rent.

2. The right tenant will always pay more for the right property and take better care of the property. "Just any tenant" will always want to pay less for any property and cause damage to the property. *Do not accept* just any tenant.

3. It is always better to have a vacancy than to have a bad tenant.

4. No matter what your gut tells you about a tenant—never trust it. In fact, in real estate management, only trust your mother. Check all tenants' records including banks, employment, previous landlords, credit records, and any other systems that are available for you to determine the pain probability (and your profitability) of this tenant.

5. Rent as if you were going to evict, and you probably will not have to.

6. Courts almost always rule in favor of the person with the most written documents.

7. Cut your losses early. Left to themselves, tenants usually go from bad to worse.

8. Long-term leases may not allow you to participate in appreciating rental rates; however, they cut down on the most expensive aspect of property management—turnover. Also, it makes a purchase through you the least costly alternative for a tenant who wants to end a lease early.

9. Consider every tenant as a potential buyer. Having them commit to long-term leases and only letting them out of the lease if they purchase a piece of real estate through you will add many dollars to the net profit of your real estate brokerage. Pay your tenants for all real estate brokerage leads.

10. Do not have preconceived ideas about how tenants from certain classes and ethnic backgrounds will behave in your rental. I have had losers from all classes and winners from all classes. Discriminate only on the basis of the applicants' ability to pay and their references. No other discrimination should ever enter into the decision-making process. We understand this in the real estate business—carry it through to your management business.

11. Never rent to anyone unless you have seen where they currently live. I do not care if they are 12 states away. If you cannot send one of your real estate agent buddies out of your local referral directory to visit their home, it is safer not to rent to them. I guarantee that your property will look exactly like their current abode within three months.

12. Minimize your expenses through preventive maintenance. Doing so always adds value to the property. There are generally several ways to make the same improvement to the property. I have discovered that the way that adds the most value to the property is always the best. Band-Aid cures end up costing you more money and usually reflect a short-term ownership mentality. Since the insider real estate acquisition policy requires long-term ownership of properties, adding value and repairing items for the long term is the most profitable method to accomplish your goals.

13. It will always cost you more to have someone else manage your property than if you manage the property yourself—unless you find a great management company. Consider how much money you make in your real estate business before you give it up to manage properties. Most property management companies charge between 6 and 10 percent of gross rent to manage your property; if you would have to sacrifice more than that amount by spending less time with your real estate business, then you should hire a management company. If you can hire someone in your own office to take care of the majority of the management duties, this would be a less expensive method. A good rule of thumb is that a management company can handle between 1 and 20 units, while you make commission income. If you have more than 20 units, it usually makes sense to hire a full-time person to take care of the management duties. This person would be your full time employee.

14. Having checklists and systems in your management business is paramount to making certain that all the i's are dotted and the t's are crossed.

In the rest of this chapter, I present some of the systems and checklists that I recommend for managing investment properties.

If you decide on outside management, a simple owner-broker management agreement (Form 18.1) is a satisfactory way to memorialize your agreement. As an insider who takes on rental properties owned by your investors, you must do a great job in management so you do not risk losing a brokerage client. If you give the management away, make certain that the management company returns any leads to you for buyers and sellers. This is an important clause to include in any agreement. Many management companies are owned and run by people with real estate licenses. If you turn over the investments of your clientele and the management company is disloyal, you may find that soon it will also be handling real estate sales for your clientele. This is why it is imperative to add a clause specifying who owns the brokerage business of the clients.

Promoting Your Rental Property

The next thing to consider is how to market your new rental property. You will do this through notices to all the other Realtors® in your board, but you will probably also use *For Rent* signs. One of your real estate brochure boxes can be used as a potential portal for flyers. The flyer should describe all the attributes, features, and benefits of the property and should include a rental application to bring to your office. I also list all the most affordable homes that I have listed for sale (who better to buy?). My sellers love this idea, and it has been responsible for five to ten sales a year.

As an insider, you probably already have a web site. Have a section for rentals on your web site, allowing users to complete and submit the rental application online. Virtual tours and other seller promotions are easy to move into the promotion of your own vacant property on your web site. A newspaper ad is still an outstanding method of renting your property, and your insider real estate rates will help cover the cost.

You need to know what leads are working the best for you and where they are coming from. I have used a traffic report (see Form 18.2) that would allow my office to monitor incoming inquiries from the Internet, telephone calls, or personal visits. It is important to find out the number of inquiries that a medium produces. Depending on the number of units I have vacant, I plan staffing to take care of inquiries. It is important also to know what is hot in your town: Are people looking for one-, two-, or three-bedroom apartments? Efficiency apartments? Furnished or unfurnished? I also track inquiries based on weather conditions. At the very end of the form, I have a section where I can enter comments about what we can do to make these properties more interesting or what additional services we can provide for the tenants.

Checking Staff Performance

On the weekend, when I had staff handling my expensive promotions to attract tenants, the results were sometimes lackluster either because my staff was poorly trained, which was my problem, or because they lacked motivation to get the unit rented—they made more money ferreting out ready, willing, and able buyers and sellers for my brokerage business.

In providing incentives to my real estate assistants, I have found triggers that motivate them to *want* to rent my apartments. I came up with a bonus system that was on a par with generating a buyer or seller lead. After I instituted the bonuses, I had testers secretly check on the staff to make certain that they were providing the customer service that I wanted for my potential tenants.

Form 18.3 is the insider rental agent performance report that I used to determine whether the agents working my phones were providing the service value that I required for tenants. You can have your tester call with questions about the vacant property. This is the document that I allowed a secret tester to use while approaching my rental agent for information. This person you use could be a friend or family member; obviously, the person needs to be unknown to the agent. The secret tester needs to keep track whether the trained rental agent asked these questions. When you use this report, you will find out exactly how hard your weekend and after-hours rental agents are working to get your property rented.

Unit Availability

It is important to have a unit availability list (Form 18.4). This document allowed my rental agents to show any of the properties that might be available or would soon be available. I always attached this list to all systems that pushed any properties for sale. I had "for sale" brochures available at board meetings, in brochure boxes, in rent notices to clients, and in my office. For all inquiries that the rental agents thought I should follow up on, we had a rental inquiry form that outlined the name, address, phones, e-mail addresses, and unit desired along with whether they might be a buyer or seller, rent desired, date desired, and the number of occupants (see Form 18.5). Sometimes my rental agent would deem it necessary for me to get involved, whether it was a buyer or seller or a person who needed to meet with me before making a decision to rent one of my properties. In that case, Form 18.5 would end up on my desk.

Qualifying Potential Tenants

Once we find potential tenants, we must determine whether they are right for our property, our life, and our future. As discussed, you will endure the most pain in renting a property by renting it to the wrong tenant. *I would rather have a vacant property than the wrong tenant.*

The potential tenant should supply you with the information needed for you to make a decision, and all occupants of the property must be disclosed. If it is at all possible, you need to check where the applicants currently live. Being an insider gives you access to a directory of the top real estate agents in the country, either through your franchise or through organizations such as CRS (Certified Research Specialists). You can use these affiliations in other states; if you have to pay someone to take an application to the potential tenants' home to determine their living standards—then do so. As mentioned, this is how your apartment will look very soon.

Let us look into the crystal ball and see if these tenants are worthy of the hard work that you have put into your rental property. . . .

The first item necessary is a check from the applicant to cover the nonrefundable fee for a credit search. You will need to find out what the credit bureau in your local area charges for a report and collect this up front from your potential tenant. Requesting a nonrefundable credit check fee goes a long way in eliminating tenants who know they have horrible credit or who are not truly interested in the unit. After you have received the fee and while you are waiting for the report, the tenant should also provide you with all personal and credit information shown in Form 18.6.

The Lease Contract

Just because tenants have given you a nonrefundable credit check fee for each occupant and have completed the application—this is no time to get lazy. Remember, you are going to be "living with" these people, giving them access to property possibly worth hundreds of thousands of dollars. You must put the right tenants in there. Please confirm all information on the application. Besides checking their credit, it may be advisable to obtain a police report, unlawful detainer reports, and all other documentation available to you through local apartment house association memberships.

Once your would-be tenants come back looking like shiny, new pennies, you are ready to enter into a long-term lease agreement with them. Many believe that taking advantage of high appreciating rental markets necessitates using month-to-month agreements. I believe that the largest expense you can have in a rental agreement is turnover. Having a long-term lease minimizes that cost.

Another great benefit of being an insider in this business is that tenants on a long-term lease sometimes change their plans because they want to buy a piece of real estate. In my lease contract (Form 18.7), tenants could void their lease obligation by using me as their real estate agent, which would allow me to earn a commission for the purchase of real estate. When I was a real estate agent and investor in

California, over 20 percent of my tenants used my services to buy real estate. We have continued that practice here in Kankakee, Illinois, by having tenants use my wife as their real estate agent of choice to avoid a lease obligation. I allow them out of my lease early with no penalties and give them every concession possible in the return of their security deposit. The tenants love this bonus, and it benefits our real estate brokerage business. It is another example of an insider benefit.

Form 18.7 is a copy of the lease contract that I use in leasing the properties that my wife and I own in Kankakee County. One caveat—this lease agreement was not written by an attorney. I have never had any problems enforcing this lease in court, but that might be a result of the quality of attorney hired by a former tenant! Before you use any contracts or forms in this book, make certain that your attorney approves them. They are included here only as samples.

Cosigner Agreements

One of the greatest benefits of being a real estate agent and investor is the number of people I meet through my tenants. Often, because a great potential tenant cannot otherwise qualify under my financial guidelines to rent one of my properties, I get to meet parents, friends, and associates. These people cosign the rental agreement to make certain that the tenant will qualify. I add their names to my real estate database for future follow-up as buyers and sellers. The number of people you meet in your real estate business determines how successful you will be in buying and selling real estate. Many times the people I have met through these cosigner agreements have turned out to be clients. Form 18.8 shows a typical cosigner agreement.

Waterbed Agreement

In your lease agreements, it is always important to include the documents that secure the conditions of your property and the use of management. One of the most serious problems I have ever had in renting properties is waterbeds or other liquid-filled furniture. Even though waterbeds are not as prevalent as they once were, they are still out there and can still cause massive damage. Form 18.9 is a copy of my waterbed agreement.

Monitoring Parking on Premises

Another major problem I have had with rentals is limiting the number of cars that can be parked on the premises. Furthermore, creating too much street traffic will result in complaints from the neighbors. I make certain that we monitor how many cars can be parked on the property by putting that notation in the lease agreement. I also keep track of the information about those cars. This helps me determine whether additional people are living in the apartment, undisclosed to me, which would allow me to charge more rent per the lease agreement. Limiting the number of people living in apartments prevents excessive wear and tear. The fastest way to determine that other people are living in a unit is by keeping track of the number of vehicles with their registration. Form 18.10 is designed to supply the necessary information.

Key Receipts

Since all my tenants receive new locks and new keys on move-in, it is imperative that we keep track of them; some properties have numerous keys for garages, mailboxes, common areas, front doors, back doors, and so on. To keep a tally of these keys, I use a key receipt for the tenants (Form 18.11). It is amazing how much time and money can be spent in the acquisition, making, and replacing of keys!

Tenants with Pets

Very few things in a rental agreement can cause more harm to a property than a pet; therefore, I make certain I know all about any pet living in one of our units. I have made it a habit to increase the security deposit substantially for a pet and must meet the pet face to face, prior to renting to a pet-owning tenant. I ask pet owners to sign the agreement stated in Form 18.12.

Once again, visiting the tenants' current residence will help determine the quality of their housekeeping and their standards of pet care.

Safety Precautions

One of the scariest aspects of owning a piece of real estate, especially when you are a large income earner as a real estate agent, is the harm that can come to people while on your premises. There is nothing more terrifying than a catastrophe happening on your property, such as a child drowning, a person being raped, or a tenant being robbed.

The first way to take care of this threat is by going to your insurance agent *today* and making certain that each property you own is covered with the correct limits. Make certain that there is a large umbrella policy covering any damages that exceed your individual policy limits. Second, you must do everything you can to maintain your property as a safe environment (e.g., have gates that self-close and lock during certain hours of the day or night). Also, have the tenants sign agreements that specify the rules and regulations. Make certain that you change the units' keys after each vacancy. Thoroughly explain alarms, smoke detectors, and all other commonsense security devices. Form 18.13 is an example of rules for a community pool.

When Tenants Leave

The preceding information will help take care of the majority of challenges in renting a property, but the biggest challenge in dealing with tenants comes when they announce that they are moving out.

The lease is expiring, and they are ready to move on with their life. If you have not turned them into a real estate client, you need to make one more presentation about the advantages of home ownership. If you are not successful and they move, not only do you have to spend time and money preparing the property for new tenants, but you also have to market the property and eat the mortgage payments. It is important to handle this transitional period in the fastest manner possible while making improvements that add long-term value to the property and are not just *Band-Aid* cures.

I first try to convince the current tenant to stay. I never accept their first request to move out. I try to use my insider knowledge and convert them to another one of my vacant properties, or I offer to make improvements to their current property, thus enticing them to stay. Remember, as an insider, you also are a great salesperson. Anything you can do to eliminate the most costly aspect of real estate ownership, the tenant turnover period, you should try to do. Finally, I try to get as much notice as possible on a possible move-out so that I can start marketing the unit and achieve a seamless transfer of tenants, with no interruption of rent payments.

If you persuade the present tenants to stay, you can send them an application for a lease renewal (Form 18.14).

Converting Tenants into Buyers

I hope that your tenants move only because they are becoming one of your buyers! I have always been proud of my ability to convert my tenants into buyers. To work toward this goal, I send them the letter shown as Form 18.15 early in their tenancy.

Managing a Move-Out

When the day comes that you are having a move-out, handle it as quickly and efficiently as possible. Form 18.16 is an insider checklist for move-outs.

Unit Make-Ready Report

After a property becomes vacant, you should fill out a checklist showing the items needing attention before the property can reach "ready to move in" status. This is a quick reference sheet for your handyman/contractor to follow in making repairs. I prefer to have all items taken care of *before* a new tenant moves in: Nothing is more annoying to tenants than discovering a lot of undone repairs when they take occupancy. It is nice to exceed their expectations on move-in, too. In fact, it is nice to exceed expectations in every aspect of your business—with buyers, sellers, tenants, and other clients. Remember, tenants are going to be some of your best buyers. Form 18.17 shows the make-ready report that I use when checking vacant units.

Keeping a Rental Record

Once the property is rented, it is wise to attach a record of that tenancy to the tenant's application and rental agreement (see Form 18.18). It makes the property worth more to an owner who might want a lender to refinance it at a lower rate. By the way, I am okay with cash-out refinancings, if you use the money to pay down another higher interest rate mortgage. Use my real estate brokerage systems to make more commission income to fund those down payments!

Move-Out Instructions

When tenants move in, be sure to include move-out instructions in the paperwork that you give them (see Form 18.19). The moment tenants decide to move out, you need to mail, e-mail, or fax this form to them again.

Taking this action will assure that the tenants recognize what is necessary for them to receive their deposit back. Since deposits are usually a large part of most tenants' down payment for a property, they want get every dollar back to facilitate their buying real estate through you. At the same time, the move-out requirements help keep units in great shape.

Maintenance of Properties

Forms 18.20 through 18.26 are necessary for keeping my properties nice and my tenants happy. They allow me to do an outstanding job of maintaining properties. When clients request their deposits back, the forms also provide a record of individual repairs made to units during their tenancy. I can determine, for example, whether a tenant's insistence that the carpets needed to be replaced way before move-out date is a legitimate claim, based on the last time that these items were repaired or replaced. All these documents will help you complete the move-out inspection completely and accurately. You will be able to uphold your great reputation as a real estate agent by being fair to your tenants.

Forms for Keeping Records

When you are just getting started in real estate management, you may not have software for keeping records. Forms 18.27 through 18.30 can help you organize your paperwork and will guide you in documenting important information. Start with these ledger reports, proceed to an Excel spreadsheet, then move on to some great software like Yardi, which is available through the Internet.

Special Communications for Tenants

It is helpful to have a residential rental questionnaire to get your tenants' perspective about important aspects of their tenancy (see Form 18.31). This information will enable you to provide service worthy of a future brokerage client. Tenants will be happy to tell you how you run your business. Keep them happy, and at the same time, keep your property nice. Likewise, when tenants cause problems for occupants of other units, let the troublemakers know immediately that the neighbors are complaining (Form 18.32).

Exit Forms

Forms 18.33, 18.34, and 18.35 are copies of my move-out letter, exit interview, and move-out closing statement. These documents add to your database of future real estate buyers and sellers. They also provide a reliable record of what the tenants liked or did not like about their tenancy as well as the disposition of the security deposit and any other monies owed. Running a business while maximizing your brokerage business is a balancing act, and business professionalism is the best way to walk that tightrope.

Downloadable FORM 18.1
Owner-Broker Management Agreement*

In consideration of the covenants herein contained, _____ hereinafter called Owner, and _____, hereinafter called broker, agrees as follows:

1. The Owner hereby employs the Broker and gives him the exclusive right to rent, lease, operate, control, and manage the following described property in _____ County, _____ upon the terms hereinafter set forth for the primate term of _____ beginning on _____.

2. Upon the expiration of the primary term of this agreement, it shall be automatically renewed and extended for a like period of time, unless either Owner or Broker shall at least thirty (30) days prior to the expiration date of such renewal term, give written notice of his desire not to renew. This agreement may be terminated at any time by mutual agreement of the parties upon payment of all commissions, fees, and expenses due hereunder to Broker. Exempting, however, the parties agree that this contract shall remain in full force and effect so long as any tenant placed in said property by Broker shall remain in possession.

3. Owner hereby makes, constitutes, and appoints Broker his true and lawful agent and attorney in fact, with power of appointment, and with authority to do and perform any and all lawful things necessary for the accomplishment of the purposes of this agreement, and:

    (a) Advertise said premises or any part thereof, to display signs thereon, and to rent same; to sign, renew, or cancel leases for the premises or any part thereof; to institute and prosecute actions to evict tenants and to recover possession of premises.

    (b) Employ and supervise all labor required for the operation and maintenance of the said premises; to make or cause to be made repairs and alteration; and to purchase necessary supplies; the Owner agreeing to assume the expenses incurred in connection therewith.

---

*Copyright © 2006 by Walter Sanford. To customize this document, download to your hard drive from www.waltersanford .com/insiderinvestingforms. The document can then be opened, edited, and printed using Microsoft Word or another popular word processing application.

(c) Collect rents due, or to become due, giving receipts therefore; and to render monthly statements to Owner of receipts, expenses, and charges and to remit receipts less disbursements; should the disbursements be in excess of the rents collected, the Owner agrees to pay such excess promptly upon demand.

(d) Broker will hold all deposits on properties and disburse on same when necessary.

(e) A late charge of $_____ will be charged when rent is _____ days late. An additional $_____ charged per day will be added until rent is paid. These late charges will be split evenly between Broker and Owner of property.

4. Owner agrees to pay Broker, as a management fee, _____% of all rents collected plus half of first months rent each year.

5. Owner agrees to indemnify and hold harmless the Broker from any claims, debts, demands, suits, costs, or charges, including necessary attorney's fees in connection with the management of the herein described property and from any liability for injury suffered on or about the premises by any employee or other person whomsoever.

6. In the event, the property of which these premises are a part is sold or exchanged by Owner or Broker, to any person, firm, or Corporation; secured or obtained by the Broker herein, during the term of this agreement, or any renewal or extension thereof, Owner shall pay the Broker a commission of _____% of the gross sales price of said property.

7. Mortgage payments to be paid by Broker.

8. In case of emergency, Owner authorizes Broker to make necessary repairs not to exceed $_____. Owner will be notified immediately whenever possible.

(continued)

This agreement shall be binding upon the successors and assigns of the Broker, and the heirs, administrators, executors, successors, and assigns the Owner. The written instrument contains all agreements between the parties, and no agreement not herein contained shall be recognized by either party. Executed this _____ day of _____, 20_____.

_____
Owner

_____
Address

_____
Phone

Downloadable FORM 18.2
Insider Traffic Report*

Week of:_____

Property:_____

Prepared by:_____

	Mon.	Tues.	Wed.	Thurs.	Fri.	Sat.	Sun.	Total
Nature of Inquiry:								
E-mail								
Telephone call								
Visitor								
Time of Inquiry:								
Morning (before 12p)								
Afternoon (12p – 5p)								
Evening (after 5p)								
Source:								
Display ad in newspaper								
Classified ad								
Billboard								
Drive-by								

*Copyright © 2006 by Walter Sanford. To customize this document, download to your hard drive from www.waltersanford .com/insiderinvestingforms. The document can then be opened, edited, and printed using Microsoft Word or another popular word processing application.

(continued)

Downloadable FORM 18.2   *(Continued)*

Internet								
Unit Desired:								
One bedroom								
Two bedroom								
Three bedroom								
Efficiency								
Furnished								
Unfurnished								
Weather Conditions								
Addresses								

Downloadable FORM 18.2   *(Continued)*

Comments:

_____

_____

_____

_____

_____

_____

_____

_____

Insider Rental Agent Performance Report*

Date: _____

Shopper: _____   Phone:_____

Rental Agent:_____   Property:_____

Yes	No	Did the agent....
❏	❏	Greet you and invite you to sit?
❏	❏	Give you his/her name?
❏	❏	Ask your name?
❏	❏	Offer to show you through a model unit or property for rent?
❏	❏	Point out features of the unit?
❏	❏	Tell you about conveniences, such as nearby shopping, schools, churches, recreational facilities, and other amenities?
❏	❏	Ask about size, family, or anticipated length of stay in area?
❏	❏	Ask your occupation and where employed?
❏	❏	Inquire as to why you chose to look at the property?
❏	❏	Show you a unit now ready for occupancy?
❏	❏	Ask why you are moving? (look for buyers and sellers!)
❏	❏	Ask where you live now?
❏	❏	Attempt to close?
❏	❏	Ask you to fill out an application?
❏	❏	Find out if you ever considered buying?
❏	❏	Ask for a deposit?
❏	❏	Ask you to rent a unit?
❏	❏	Continue to sell after you said you had not yet decided? How many times?
❏	❏	Attempt to get your phone number and e-mail address?
❏	❏	Ask if you had any real estate for sale?
❏	❏	Appear sincere and interested in you?
❏	❏	Give you a brochure or handout?

*Copyright © 2006 by Walter Sanford. To customize this document, download to your hard drive from www.waltersanford.com/insiderinvestingforms. The document can then be opened, edited, and printed using Microsoft Word or another popular word processing application.

❏   ❏   Have a pleasant personality and attitude?

❏   ❏   Appear knowledgeable?

❏   ❏   Use good phrasing and have easily understood diction?

❏   ❏   Refer you to another property?

❏   ❏   Indicate the number of vacant units?

Did you make other observations that might be important, and if so, what were they? _____

_____

_____

_____

Give an overall rating of the agent on a 1 (poor) to 10 (excellent) scale _____.

Downloadable FORM 18.4
Unit Availability List*

Property:_____   Date:_____

Address	Unit No.	Bed Bath	Color Scheme	$ Rent	Vacating Date	Ready to Show	Lease Term	Special Features or Remarks

*Copyright © 2006 by Walter Sanford. To customize this document, download to your hard drive from www.waltersanford .com/insiderinvestingforms. The document can then be opened, edited, and printed using Microsoft Word or another popular word processing application.

Downloadable FORM 18.5

Rental Inquiry*

Name: _____

Address: _____ Phone: _____

E-mail address: _____

Place Employed: _____ Phone: _____

Unit Desired: _____

Might be: ☐ Buyer   ☐ Seller

Rent Desired: $_____ Date Desired: _____

How Many Occupants and Relationship: _____

Unit Shown: _____ Rent Quoted: $_____

Follow-up Remarks: _____

_____

Date Inquiry Received: _____ Inquiry Taken by: _____

Reason they need to speak with Walter: _____

_____

_____

*Copyright © 2006 by Walter Sanford. To customize this document, download to your hard drive from www.waltersanford .com/insiderinvestingforms. The document can then be opened, edited, and printed using Microsoft Word or another popular word processing application.

Downloadable FORM 18.6
Tenant's Personal and Credit Information*

Anticipated length of occupancy:_____

Personal Data

Name:_____ Date of Birth:_____

Social Security No.: _____ Driver's License No.: _____

Name:_____ Date of Birth:_____

Social Security No.: _____ Driver's License No.: _____

Present Address: _____

How Long at Present Address:_____ Landlord/Agent:_____

Residence Phone:_____ Business Phone:_____

Landlord/Agent Business Phone: _____

Past Address: _____ How Long:_____

Landlord/Agent:_____ Business Phone:_____

Occupants:

Name:_____ Relationship:_____ Age:_____

Name:_____ Relationship:_____ Age:_____

Name:_____ Relationship:_____ Age:_____

Name:_____ Relationship:_____ Age:_____

Pets? (include type, size, and age):_____

Car Make/Year/Model/Color/License No.: _____

*Copyright © 2006 by Walter Sanford. To customize this document, download to your hard drive from www.waltersanford .com/insiderinvestingforms. The document can then be opened, edited, and printed using Microsoft Word or another popular word processing application.

Occupation

	Present Occupation*	Prior Occupation*	Cotenant's Occupation
Occupation			
Employer			
Self-employed, doing business as			
Business Address			
Business Phone			
Type of Business			
Position Held			
Superior's Name and Title			
How Long			
Monthly Gross Income			

*If employed or self-employed less than two years, give some information on prior occupation.

Notes of explanation:_____

_____

_____

(continued)

Downloadable FORM 18.6   *(Continued)*

References

Bank Reference		Address			Phone
Credit Reference	Account No.	Address	Highest Amount Owed	Purpose of Credit	Account Open or Date Closed

Personal Reference	Address	Phone	Length of Acquaintance	Occupation

Nearest Relative (Name)	Address	Phone	City	Relationship

Have you ever filed a petition in bankruptcy?_____

Have you ever been evicted from any tenancy?_____

When would you consider buying a home? We can offer many benefits. _____

_____

If positive to the above, what would you be looking for? _____

_____

_____

_____

Have you ever willfully and intentionally refused to pay any rent when due? _____

I declare the foregoing to be true under penalty of perjury.

I agree that any agreement entered into in reliance on my misstatement made above may be voidable by the landlord.

Applicant:_____ Dated:_____

Address:_____

Applicant:_____ Dated:_____

Address:_____

Key Deposit: $_____

Security Deposit: $_____

Other Costs/Fees: $_____

Total: $_____

In the event that this agreement is not accepted by the Owner or his authorized agent, within _____ days, the total deposit less the credit check fee received shall be refunded.

Tenant hereby offers to rent from the Owner the premises situated in the City of _____, County of_____, State of _____, described as _____ upon the following TERMS and CONDITIONS:

TERM: The proposed term hereof shall commence on _____, 20_____, and continue until_____,

Downloadable FORM 18.7
Sanford Systems Lease Contract*

THIS AGREEMENT, Made this _____ day of
_____, **20**_____, between _____,
Lesse(s) (names) and **Walter** and **Lisa Sanford** Lessors.

WITNESSETH, That Sanford does hereby lease to the said Lessee(s), the following described property, situated in the County of **Kankakee** State of **Illinois** to be used only as a **personal residence**. Its exact address being:
_____, _____, IL _____.

For the term of **two years** beginning on the _____ day of _____, **20**_____, and ending on the _____ day of _____, **20**_____.

And the tenant agrees to pay as rent for the said premises, the sum of _____ DOLLARS payable in advance on the **1st** day of each month, at **559 South Washington Avenue, Kankakee, IL 60901**.

SUMMARY OF LEASE:

A. Beginning Date: _____

B. Rent Per Month: _____

   1. Total Rent over term of lease: _____

C. Day of Month Rent Due: **1st (first)**

   Day Rent is Late: **6th (sixth)**

D. Late Rent Charge: **10% of rent payment**

E. Security Deposit: _____

F. Utilities Provided: **None**

G. Parking: _____

H. Storage: _____

I. (1)Maximum number Occupants per agreement: _____

   (2) Maximum number occupants per law: _____

J. Named Tenant: _____
_____

   Children: _____
_____

K. Added Tenant Rent: **$100**

L. Water Bed: _____

   Musical Instruments: _____

M. Charitable Organization: _____

N. Personal Property Owned by Lessor: _____

1. The tenant is responsible for all payments of utilities, lawn maintenance, and snow removal.
2. Rent is due on the **1st** of each month. If rent is not received by the **5th**, it is considered late with a late charge of **10% of your rent payment.**

Initials   ___ ___ ___ ___

*Copyright © 2006 by Walter Sanford. To customize this document, download to your hard drive from www.waltersanford.com/insiderinvestingforms. The document can then be opened, edited, and printed using Microsoft Word or another popular word processing application.

3. Failure of Lessee to pay the rent or other charges due hereunder or to comply with any of the covenants or conditions herein contained shall, at **Sanford's** option, forthwith terminate this Lease and Lessee's rights therein as provided by law.

4. In the event of Lessee's failure to give such notice of intention to terminate, he/she shall be liable for another full term.

5. Failure by **Sanford** to exercise any right under this Agreement or acceptance of rent after default by Lessee shall not be deemed to waive such default or to affect any notice theretofore given, or legal proceeding theretofore commenced.

6. Lessee agrees that he will not without **Sanford's** consent in writing endorsed hereon, bring upon, keep, maintain, or permit to be kept or maintained, in, on, or upon the premises any additional dog, cat, parrot, or other animal. This will immediately increase security deposit another **$1,000**, payable on same day unauthorized animal is housed, chained, or stored on the property.

7. Lessee agrees that he/she will not, without **Sanford's** consent in writing endorsed hereon, bring upon, keep, maintain, or permit to be kept or maintained, in, on, or upon the premises any waterbeds, or liquid-filled furniture.

8. The house shall be used and occupied by Lessees exclusively as a private, single-family residence. Neither the house nor any part of the house or yard shall be used at anytime during the term of this lease for the purpose of carrying on business, profession, or trade of any kind, or for any purpose other than as a private single-family residence. Lessee shall comply with all the health and sanitary laws, ordinances, rules, and orders of appropriate government authorities, if any, with respect to the house.

9. Lessee agrees not to violate any law, statute, or ordinance, nor to commit, suffer or permit any waste, or nuisance in, on, or about the said premises.

10. Lessee agrees not to alter the premises whatsoever without **Sanford's** permission in writing.

11. Lessee shall not keep or have on or around the house any article or thing of a dangerous, inflammable, or explosive character that might unreasonably increase the danger of fire on or around the house or that might be considered hazardous.

12. Lessee shall be responsible for maintaining the cleanliness of drapes, curtains, mini-blinds, and carpets if applicable.

13. If any legal action or proceeding be brought by either party to enforce any part of this Agreement, the prevailing party shall recover, in addition to all other relief, actual attorney's fees and costs.

14. **Sanford** reserves the right to himself or his agent to enter said premises in case of emergency, to make necessary or agreed repairs, decorations, alterations or improvements, supplying necessary or agreed services or exhibit the dwelling to prospective purchasers, mortgagees, tenants, workmen or contractors or any tenant who has abandoned or surrendered the premises or pursuant to court order. Except in cases of emergency or abandonment, entry will be made during normal business hours. Or in case it is impractical to do so, landlord shall give the tenant reasonable notice of intent to enter, no less than 24 hours. Lessee agrees not to change any lock or locking device to said premises without the prior written consent of **Sanford**, but Lessee will on demand furnish **Sanford** with keys and four copies as duplicates.

15. **Sanford** shall not be liable or responsible in any way for injury to any person, or for loss of, or damage to, any article belonging to Lessee located in said premises, or other premises under control of lessee. No right of storage is given by this Agreement. **Sanford** shall not be liable for nondelivery or misdelivery of messages nor shall **Sanford** be liable for and this Agreement shall not be terminated by reason of any interruption of, or interference with, services or accommodation due Lessee, caused by strike, riot, orders of public authorities, acts of other Lessees, accident, the making of necessary repairs to the building of which said premises are a part, or any other cause beyond **Sanford's** control.

Initials   ___ ___ ___ ___

(continued)

16. The undersigned Lessee(s) whether or not in actual possession of premises, are jointly and severally liable for all rent incurred during the term of this Agreement, and for all damages to the demised premises caused or permitted by residents, their guests and invitees.

17. Nothing herein contained shall be construed to grant Lessee any right to enter upon any portion of the roof of said premises for any purposes whatsoever without **Sanford's** consent in writing first hand and obtained, NOR SHALL LESSEE ENTER INTO A CONTRACTUAL AGREEMENT WITH A CABLE TV OR SATELLITE COMPANY.

18. Lessee covenants that he/she will occupy the premises continuously, except for normal vacation periods, and agrees that any absence for more than 14 days during any part of which time rent is delinquent shall be conclusively presumed to be an abandonment of the premises.

19. It is understood by Lessee and all parties that Lessee's personal effects are not insured by **Sanford** and that Lessee may insure his own personal property with his/her own tenant insurance policy.

20. Lessee shall not store boats, camper trailers, large trucks, or motor homes on or near the subject property.

21. Lessee acknowledges that **Sanford** does not provide a security alarm system or any security for the house or for the Lessee and that any such alarm or security device, if provided, is not represented or warranted to be complete in all respects or to protect Lessee from all harm. Lessee hereby releases **Sanford** from any loss, suit, claim, charge, damage, or injury resulting from lack of security or failure of security.

22. Lessee shall deposit with the owner, as a Security Deposit, the sum of **$1,000**, payable upon occupancy. **Sanford** may claim (withhold) of the Security Deposit only such amounts as reasonably necessary to remedy Lessee defaults as follows:

    a. to repair damages to the premises caused by Lessee, exclusive of ordinary wear and tear or,

    b. to clean such premises if necessary, upon termination of the tenancy, or

    c. to fumigate.

    Not later than two weeks (14 days) after the Lessee has vacated the premises, **Sanford** shall furnish the Lessee with any itemized written statement of the basis for, and the amount of, any security withheld or amounts beyond the withheld security deposit and shall return any remaining portion of such security to the Lessee. Total of all deposits not to exceed two (2) months rent for an unfurnished or three (3) months for furnished unit. Lessee is responsible for amount of money required in *a, b,* and *c* above that exceeds security deposit.

23. The premises are equipped with Smoke Detection device(s) and:

    a. The Lessee acknowledges that the Smoke Detector(s) was tested and its operation explained by **Sanford** or **Sanford's agent** in the presence of the Lessee at the time of initial occupancy and that the Smoke Detector(s) were in proper working order at the time.

    b. Each Lessee shall perform the manufacturer's recommended test to determine if the Smoke Detector(s) is/are operating properly at least once a week.

    c. INITIAL ONLY IF BATTERY OPERATED: By initialing as provided, each Lessee understands that said Smoke Detector(s) and Alarm is a battery-operated unit and it shall be each Lessee's responsibility to:

Initials   ___ ___ ___ ___

1. Ensure that the battery is in operating condition at all times.

2. Replace the battery as needed (unless otherwise provided by law).

3. If, after replacing the battery, the Smoke Detector(s) do not work, inform **Sanford** or Lessor's Agent immediately _____ _____ _____ _____ .

d. Lessee(s) must inform **Sanford** or **Sanford's agent** immediately, in writing, of any defect malfunction or failure of any detector(s).

e. If law requires that **Sanford** test the Smoke Detector(s), the Lessee shall allow **Sanford** or **Sanford's agent** access to the premises for that purpose.

24. Furnace has been serviced and a new filter installed. The filter size for this home is _____ x _____. Filters need to be replaced every six months for the health of the Lessee and to keep the furnace running as efficient as possible. It is in the Lessee's best financial interest to replace the filters every six months. Not replacing the filters in a biyearly manner is a violation of this lease and Lessee agrees to pay for any damage caused to the furnace by not replacing the filters.

25. Lessee shall not transfer his interest in or to this Agreement, nor shall Lessee assign or sublet said premises nor any part hereof. ANY ATTEMPT TO SUBLET OR ASSIGN SHALL BE VOID AND AN IRREMEDIABLE BREACH OF THIS AGREEMENT.

26. ATTACHMENTS: By initialing as provided, Lessee acknowledges receipt of those indicated attachments, copy(s) of which is/are attached hereto, marked by indicated page number(s) and are incorporated herein as though fully set forth at length. Each Lessee should initial each attachment.

a. Cosigner Agreement attached marked as page(s) _____ Initial (   )

b. Inventory which describes the furnishing(s) of premises marked as page(s) _____ Initial (   )

c. Waterbed/Liquid Filled Furniture Agreement marked as page(s)_____ Initial (   )

d. Lead Paint Disclosure marked as page(s) _____ Initial (   )

e. Addendum(s) marked as page(s) _____ Initial (   )

27. Personal property included, owned by _____ and included in lease for Lessee's use. Lessee to be responsible for all maintenance, and repair. Lessee to relinquish control and deliver up the following personal property at the end of the lease in the same condition as provided at the beginning of the lease. _____

If appliances have been replaced by the Lessee, then the Lessee is to remove the appliances at the end of the tenancy or give lessor first right of refusals to purchase.

28. **This is a non-smoking home.** Lessee understands that smoking or burning candles in the home is prohibited, unless otherwise arranged with an additional deposit of $_____ for a total deposit amount of $_____. Lessee also agrees to provide proper containment of cigarette butts, so not to litter outside of property. **Initial** ____ ____ ____ ____

29. **Lease can be broken at any time, without penalty, if tenant makes a real estate purchase using Lisa Sanford as their exclusive agent.**

30. Maximum number of permanent resident vehicles parked on or around premises: _____

31. Other: _____

Initials   ___ ___ ___ ___

(continued)

Downloadable FORM 18.7   *(Continued)*

Total Received: _____ Check # _____

Balance due of _____ on or before _____,
20_____.

The undersigned Lessee(s) acknowledges having read and understood the foregoing
and receipt of a duplicate original.

Dated this _____ day of_____, **20**_____.

_____   _____
            Owner   Lessee

_____   _____
            Owner   Lessee

                        Initials   ___   ___   ___   ___

Addendum A

Congratulations on the lease of your new home! You should have a copy of your lease agreement. If not, please don't hesitate to contact our office for one.

Be sure you meet with your insurance agent prior to moving in so they will have time to prepare the necessary renter's contents policy. My insurance does not cover your belongings.

For your convenience, we have put a check next to the utility companies that you will want to contact before moving in so you can receive heat, water, trash, phone, and mandatory Kankakee sticker if you reside in Kankakee.

- ❑ Com Ed (electric) 1-800-334-7661

- ❑ SBC 1-800-244-4444

- ❑ Nicor (gas) 1-888-642-6748

- ❑ Consumer Water 935-8803 (water and trash for Kankakee residents)

- ❑ Trash pick-up ABC Disposal 932-2911 or Action 935-7401 Apollo 472-4111

- ❑ Bradley Sewer 932-4679

- ❑ Bourbonnais Sewer 933-1676

- ❑ The *Daily Journal* 937-3300 The *Herald-Country Market* 933-1131

- ❑ Cable service AT&T Broadband 1-866-594-1234 (Get approval from **Sanford** for installation)

If you have any questions, please call. Thanks again for your business!

Sincerely,

Walter S. Sanford

Phone 815.929.9258

Received by _____   _____

Initials   ____ ____ ____ ____

(continued)

Addendum B: **Disclosure of Information and Acknowledgment**

Lead-Based Paint and/or Lead-Based Paint Hazards

Lead Warning Statement

Every purchaser of any interest in residential real property on which a residential dwelling was built prior to 1978 is notified that such property may present exposure to lead from lead-based paint that may place young children at risk of developing lead poisoning. Lead poisoning in young children may produce permanent neurological damage, including learning disabilities, reduced intelligence quotient, behavioral problems, and impaired memory. Lead poisoning also poses a particular risk to pregnant women. The seller of any interest in residential real property is required to provide the buyer with any information on lead-based paint hazards from risk assessments or inspections in the seller's possession and notify the buyer of any known lead-based paint hazards. A risk assessment or inspection for possible lead-based paint hazards is recommended prior to purchase.

Lessor's Disclosure (initial): All lessees should initial.

_____ (a) Presence of lead-based paint and/or lead-based paint hazards (check one below):

_____ ❏ Known lead-based paint and/or lead-based paint hazards are present in the housing (explain): _____

_____

_____ ❏ Lessor has no knowledge of lead-based paint and/or lead-based hazards in the housing.

_____ (b) Records and reports available to the lessee (check one below):

_____ ❏ Lessor has provided the purchaser with all available records and reports pertaining to lead-based paint and/or lead-based hazards in the housing (list documents below):

_____

_____

_____ ❏ Lessor has no reports or records pertaining to lead-based paint and/or lead-based hazards in the housing.

Lessor's Acknowledgment (initial): All lessees should initial.

_____ (c) Lessee has received copies of all information listed above.

_____ (d) Lessee has received the pamphlet *Protect Your Family from Lead in Your Home.*

Initials   ____ ____ ____ ____

_____ (e) Lessee has (check one below):

_____ ❏ Received a 10-day opportunity (or mutually agreed upon period) to conduct a risk assessment or inspection of the presence of lead-based paint or lead-based paint hazards; or

_____ ❏ Waived the opportunity to conduct a risk assessment or inspection for the presence of lead-based paint and/or lead-based hazards.

Agent's Acknowledgment (initial): lessee's designated agent

_____ (f) Agent has informed the seller of the seller's obligations under 42 U. S. C. 4852D and is aware of his/her responsibility to ensure compliance.

Certification of Accuracy

The following parties have reviewed the information above and certify, to the best of their knowledge, that the information they have provided is true and accurate.

Lessor: _____ Date: _____/_____/_____

Lessor: _____ Date: _____/_____/_____

Lessor's Agent: _____ Date: _____/_____/_____

Lessee: _____ Date: _____/_____/_____

Lessee: _____ Date: _____/_____/_____

Lessee's Agent: _____ Date: _____/_____/_____

Location of property: _____

City: _____ State: _____

Zip: _____

Initials ___ ___ ___ ___

Downloadable FORM 18.8

Cosigner Agreement Addendum to Rental Agreement*

My name is _____, and I understand that this

agreement is attached to and forms a part of the Rental Agreement between

_____, Lessor and _____,

Lessee(s), for the property located at _____

and which is dated the _____ day of _____,

20_____.

I have completed a rental application for the express purpose of enabling the Lessor
to check my credit. I have no intention of occupying the dwelling as described in
the rental agreement referred to.

I have read the rental agreement referred to, and I promise to guarantee the
Lessee(s) compliance with the financial obligations of this agreement.

I understand that I may be required to pay for rent, cleaning charges, or damage
assessments in such amounts as are incurred by the Lessee(s) under the terms of
this agreement if, and only if, the Lessee(s) fail to pay.

_____	_____
Name	Date

Address:_____

Phone:_____

_____	_____
Name	Date

Address:_____

Phone:_____

*Copyright © 2006 by Walter Sanford. To customize this document, download to your hard drive from www.waltersanford
.com/insiderinvestingforms. The document can then be opened, edited, and printed using Microsoft Word or another popular word processing application.

Waterbed and/or Liquid-Filled Furniture Agreement*

This agreement is entered into this _____ day of _____, 20_____,

by and between _____, "Owner" (Landlord)

and _____, "Resident" (Tenant).

In consideration of their mutual promises, the parties agree as follows:

1. Resident is renting from Owner the premises located at: _____

    _____

2. Resident has informed Owner that the following water(s) and/or liquid-filled furniture will be used in the premises and is hereinafter referred to as "said items":

    _____

    _____

3. Consent to use waterbed(s) or liquid-filled furniture in the premises is given, subject to the terms of this agreement.

4. Resident agrees to furnish to Owner, prior to installation of "said items," a valid waterbed insurance policy or certificate of insurance for property damage, having a minimum policy limit of $200,000. The policy shall be issued by a company licensed to do business in California and possessing a Best's Insurance Report rating of "B" or higher. The policy shall cover replacement value of all property damage, including loss of use, incurred by the Owner or others caused by or a rising out of the ownership, maintenance, use, or removal of the waterbed or liquid-filled furniture until waterbed or liquid-filled furniture is permanently removed from the rental premises. The Owner may require the resident to produce evidence of insurance at any time. Resident understands that the insurance carrier is to give the Owner 10 days prior written notice of cancellation, nonrenewal, lapse or change in the insurance policy.

5. The Resident agrees to comply with the minimum component specification list prescribed by the manufacturer, retailer, or state law, whichever provides the higher degree of safety. The Resident agrees to install, maintain and remove "said items" according to standard methods of installation, maintenance, and removal as prescribed by the manufacturer, retailer, or state law, whichever provides the higher degree of safety.

    Cost of installation is the responsibility of Resident. The Resident shall notify the Owner in writing of the intent to install, remove, or move the waterbed or liquid-filled furniture. The notice shall be delivered at least twenty-four hours prior to the installation, removal, or movement. The Owner maybe present at the time of installation, removal, or movement at the Owner's option. If "said items" are installed or moved by any person other than the Resident, the Resident shall deliver to the Owner a written installation receipt stating the installer's name, address, and business affiliation where appropriate. Any installation or movement of "said items" shall conform to the Owner's reasonable structural specifications for placement within the rental property and shall be consistent with floor capacity of the rental dwelling unit.

---

*Copyright © 2006 by Walter Sanford. To customize this document, download to your hard drive from www.waltersanford .com/insiderinvestingforms. The document can then be opened, edited, and printed using Microsoft Word or another popular word processing application.

(continued)

6. Resident shall be liable to Owner for all damages and expenses incurred by or in connection with "said items," and shall hold Owner harmless for any and all damages and costs in connection therewith. As additional security, Resident agrees to pay Owner the sum of $_____ (receipt of which is hereby acknowledged). If a heater is provided by Resident and Owner pays for the utilities for said heater, Resident shall pay Owner the sum of $_____ per month on each rent payment date, as a special payment (not to be construed as rent) for the added utility costs.

7. Upon reasonable notice, Owner may enter the premises to inspect "said items" upon completion of installation and periodically thereafter. In an emergency, to prevent injury or damage, Resident agrees to immediately remove "said items." If Resident fails to do so, Owner may remove "said items" at Resident's expense.

8. Resident agrees to comply with all the requirements of:

   (a) Governing building codes;

   (b) Health and Safety Code; and

   (c) All other applicable governmental laws and regulations.

9. This agreement is an addendum and part of the Rental Agreement and/or Lease between Owner and Resident. In the event of default by Resident of any of the terms, Resident agrees, within three days after receiving written notice of default from Owner, to cure the default or vacate the premises.

_____	_____
Resident	Date
_____	_____
Resident	Date
_____	_____
Owner Agent	Date

Downloadable FORM 18.10
Vehicle Registration*

Vehicle License Number: _____

Property Address: _____

Occupant's Name(s): _____

Unit No.: _____ Phone: _____

Make of Vehicle: _____

Year:_____ Color:_____

Operator's Driver's License No.: _____

State of Vehicle Registry: _____

A separate registration form must be filled out for each vehicle.

Occupant's Signature: _____

Date: _____

*Copyright © 2006 by Walter Sanford. To customize this document, download to your hard drive from www.waltersanford .com/insiderinvestingforms. The document can then be opened, edited, and printed using Microsoft Word or another popular word processing application.

Downloadable FORM 18.11
Key Receipt*

Property Address: _____

Occupant's Name(s): _____

Unit:_____ Phone:_____

The undersigned hereby acknowledges receipt of the following keys:

No. of Keys   Serial Numbers, if applicable

_____   Apartment/House   _____

_____   Mailbox   _____

_____   _____   _____

_____   _____   _____

_____   _____
Occupant's Signature   Date

*Copyright © 2006 by Walter Sanford. To customize this document, download to your hard drive from www.waltersanford .com/insiderinvestingforms. The document can then be opened, edited, and printed using Microsoft Word or another popular word processing application.

Lease Agreement for Pet Owners*

1. This agreement made on the _____ day of _____, 20_____, by and between _____ acting herein through is duly authorized agent, herein described as Landlord and _____, herein described as Tenant, whereby:

2. Owner gives resident permission to house the pet described below on the premises leased by Owner under the terms of:

   Lease agreement dated the _____ day of _____, 20_____, upon the following conditions:

   (a) Tenant agrees that no additional or different pet will occupy the premises, even temporarily, under this agreement; that tenant will execute a separate pet lease agreement for each pet that occupies the premises under the above described lease agreement.

   (b) Tenant agrees that if pet becomes annoying, bothersome, or in any way a nuisance to other residents Tenant will immediately upon notice from the Owner, remove the pet from the premises or vacate the premises.

   (c) Tenant agrees to deposit with Owner upon execution of this pet lease agreement the sum of $_____; said deposit is in addition to the security deposit required and paid under the above described lease agreement, and subject to the same terms and conditions.

   Type of Pet:_____   Breed:_____

   Name of Pet:_____   Age:_____ Color:_____

3. Executed this the _____ day of _____, 20_____; this agreement to be attached to and become a part of the above described lease agreement.

   Resident:_____   Landlord:_____

   Resident:_____   Date:_____

*Copyright © 2006 by Walter Sanford. To customize this document, download to your hard drive from www.waltersanford .com/insiderinvestingforms. The document can then be opened, edited, and printed using Microsoft Word or another popular word processing application.

Pool Rules and Regulations*

1. The pool is to be used only between the hours of _____a.m. and _____ p.m.

2. The pool is reserved exclusively for use of residents of the building. Guests can use the pool only with express prior permission from management.

3. Children under the age of 14 shall not use pool without an adult in attendance.

4. Any person known to be, or suspected of being afflicted with an infectious disease, suffering from a cough, cold, or sores, or wearing bandages shall be excluded from using all pool facilities unless such person submits a written statement, signed by a licensed physician, confirming that the person does not present a health hazard to other pool users, or permission is given by the management.

5. No food may be served or eaten in or around the pool area at any time, without management's consent. Refreshments must be served in unbreakable containers.

6. No alcoholic beverages shall be served or drunk in or around the pool area at any time. No person under the influence of alcoholic beverages is permitted in or near the pool.

7. Running and jumping, "horseplay," fighting, boisterous or dangerous conduct, and/or any noisy behavior disturbing to the other tenants, is forbidden in or around the pool area.

8. No radios, record players, or other musical instruments may be used in or around the pool area without consent of management.

9. Residents and their guests are required to be properly attired at all times, going to and from and in or around the pool area.

10. Showering is required prior to using the pool. Those using the pool shall dry themselves off before leaving the pool area.

11. Residents and guests will place their own towels over pool furniture when using suntan oil or other lotions.

*Copyright © 2006 by Walter Sanford. To customize this document, download to your hard drive from www.waltersanford.com/insiderinvestingforms. The document can then be opened, edited, and printed using Microsoft Word or another popular word processing application.

12. No toys, inner tubes, or any other objects whatsoever will be allowed in the pool at any time.

13. Safety equipment is not to be used except in case of an emergency.

14. NO LIFEGUARD WILL BE ON DUTY. Persons using pool facilities do so at their own risk. Management assumes no responsibility for accident or injury. Management is not responsible for articles lost, damaged, or stolen.

NOTE: This does not waive Owner's duty of care to prevent personal injury or property damage where that duty is imposed by law.

The undersigned Resident(s) acknowledge(s) having read and understood the foregoing, and receipt of a duplicate original.

_____   _____
           Resident   Resident

Downloadable FORM 18.14
Application for Lease Renewal*

Name(s) of <u>ALL</u> Adult Tenants: _____

_____

_____

Address of Premises: _____

Daytime Phone: _____ Evening Phone: _____

E-mail address:_____

Have there been any changes to your employment or income since your last rental

application was submitted?   Yes   No

If so, please indicate below:_____

_____

_____

Do you have (or plan to have) liquid-filled furniture?   Yes   No

If so, please describe: _____

_____

Have you obtained any animals?   Yes   No

If so, please describe: _____

_____

Have you changed any locks?   Yes   No

If so, please describe: _____

_____

Changes to original lease agreement: _____

_____

All other terms of the lease agreement dated _____ shall remain in full
force and effect.

_____   _____
           Signature   Date

*Copyright © 2006 by Walter Sanford. To customize this document, download to your hard drive from www.waltersanford .com/insiderinvestingforms. The document can then be opened, edited, and printed using Microsoft Word or another popular word processing application.

Buyer Lead Generation to Your Tenant*

Date

Name
Address
City, State Zip

Name:

It has been a pleasure to supply your housing needs. It is my goal to service you in any real estate realm. In fact, I'm a successful real estate broker fulfilling many buyers' dreams. The time may come where you dream about owning your own home, and I want to let you know that I can make it as easy as possible for you. You might ask why I would possibly want to lose a wonderful tenant? The answer is, if I am going to lose a tenant, the only way I want to lose one is by making that person one of my happy buyers.

Here is the plan of action that I have for my tenants who have become buyers in the past. If you use me as your real estate agent, you can expect the following:

1. I will apply double the amount of your security deposit toward your down payment. This only applies, however, if your full security deposit is refundable and there is no damage done to the premises.

2. I will introduce you to some of the best service providers in Long Beach. You will be treated to the best lender in town who, because of my volume, will offer you the best rates and terms. This lender will also prequalify you so that all mystery is removed from how much of a loan you can afford and what your payments will be.

3. I can arrange a fifteen-minute free interview with my accountant, so that you can determine the change in your tax status once you own your home.

4. I will introduce you to the very best in home inspection people so that for a very small sum we will know every potential problem that can be cured prior to you moving into your new home.

5. I will introduce you to insurance people, title people, escrow people, and others who will make this transaction extremely smooth.

6. I will allow you to break your lease with no penalties.

---

*Copyright © 2006 by Walter Sanford. To customize this document, download to your hard drive from www.waltersanford .com/insiderinvestingforms. The document can then be opened, edited, and printed using Microsoft Word or another popular word processing application.

(continued)

As you can see, I've done this before—moving people from rentals to ownership. One of the reasons I like this business so much is that many of my clients, prior to an initial consultation, did not realize that they could own their own home; therefore they are reaping the benefits of a lifetime from their eventual purchase. I would like to offer you that initial consultation now.

Please call me if you're thinking of buying a home for yourself or your family. Oh by the way, it doesn't necessarily have to be in this town. If it isn't, I understand; I cannot offer you the advantage of doubling your security deposit, but what I can offer you is a referral to the best agent in any city in the world.

Please consider your future and let me know how I can play a part in the real estate part of it.

Sincerely,

Walter Sanford
Sanford Systems

Insider Rental Checklist for Move-Outs*

As soon as tenant gives notice:

Close for them to be the buyer.

Negotiate renewal of lease.

Look at rental comps.

Check interior and exterior condition of property.

Put up rental sign in window.

Put rental sign in yard.

Place lockbox on property.

Write and place ad in newspaper and web site (virtual tour also).

Put rental into real estate agent blast and make hard copy for rental book.

Call rental companies and inform them of pending vacancy.

Pay a "bounty" for good tenants referred by existing tenants.

As soon as property becomes vacant:

Contact adjacent neighbors for security.

Turn on all utilities and record in log book.

Make arrangements for watering of lawn, if necessary.

Hire a lawn service to mow during vacancy.

Do all necessary repairs to property.

Have property cleaned, carpets shampooed, drapes cleaned.

Check on completion of repairs.

When property is rented:

Complete all paperwork with tenant and obtain deposits.

Remove window and yard rental signs.

Remove lockbox and tag key. Return it to office key board.

Remove rental from computer and rental book.

Check finish time on repairs.

---

*Copyright © 2006 by Walter Sanford. To customize this document, download to your hard drive from www.waltersanford .com/insiderinvestingforms. The document can then be opened, edited, and printed using Microsoft Word or another popular word processing application.

(continued)

When new tenants move into property:

Turn over utilities and record in log book.

Discontinue lawn service.

Discontinue pool service.

Collect balance of tenant's money, give keys to tenants, and an inspection form to be returned within 72 hours.

Change all records to reflect new tenants.

Call adjacent neighbors to inform and thank them.

Downloadable FORM 18.17
Unit Make-Ready Report*

Property: _____

Unit: _____   Type: _____

Date Vacated: _____   Date to Be Occupied: _____

Inspection by: _____   Date: _____

Checklist before Move-In	Instructions
Check all plumbing (toilets, faucets, all plumbing in unit). Make sure no leaks.	
Check all appliances (run dishwasher once on each cycle, check for proper operation of refrigerator, disposal, and range).	
Check hardware in unit (all doorknobs, closet hooks, closet rods, door pulls, night locks, door stops, magnetic catches, etc.).	
Check blinds for proper operation.	
Check all walls for holes, seams, cuts, nail pops.	
Check paint (all walls, ceilings, woodwork, trim that need to be cleaned or painted; no spots, streaks, or scratches).	
Check flooring (all floors cleaned and waxed, parquet block floors or wood strip and asphalt tile included; carpet vacuumed).	
Bathroom(s) cleaned (tubs, toilets, tile walls, tile floor, vanities, mirrors, medicine cabinets, and sinks clean).	
All towel bars, toilet paper holders, soap dishes installed and cleaned.	
Check tile in bathroom(s) for cracks or flaws.	

*Copyright © 2006 by Walter Sanford. To customize this document, download to your hard drive from www.waltersanford .com/insiderinvestingforms. The document can then be opened, edited, and printed using Microsoft Word or another popular word processing application.

(continued)

Downloadable FORM 18.17   *(Continued)*

Checklist before Move-In	Instructions
All baseboards, shelves in closet, electrical outlet plates installed properly.	
All thresholds and metal strips installed where needed.	
Check that all doors close properly, with no rubbing or warping.	
Check that all vents and registers are installed.	
Check heating and air conditioning (when appropriate) to be sure working properly.	
Check that new filters are installed in all air handling units or air-conditioning units (when appropriate).	
Make sure there are no odors in the property.	
All kitchen cabinets cleaned inside and outside.	
Windows cleaned.	
Check all lighting (new bulbs in all fixtures, and all fixtures hung and working).	
Check for landscaping weeds, oil stains, and garage cleanliness.	
Make certain that all locks are changed. All window locks work along with fire and burglar alarms.	

Final Inspection by: _____   Date: _____

Approved by: _____   Date: _____

Downloadable FORM 18.18
Rental Record*

Address: _____

Property was placed into service as a rental unit on: _____

Date: _____ Number of Units: _____

Draw diagram of units:

Floor 1   Floor 2   Floor 3

Appliances/Furnishings:

Unit No.: _____   Unit No.: _____

Item _____ Value _____   Item _____ Value _____

_____ _____   _____ _____

_____ _____   _____ _____

_____ _____   _____ _____

Unit No.: _____   Unit No.: _____

Item _____ Value _____   Item _____ Value _____

_____ _____   _____ _____

_____ _____   _____ _____

_____ _____   _____ _____

Breakdown of property for writing values off at different rates.

Land value: _____

Building value: _____

*Copyright © 2006 by Walter Sanford. To customize this document, download to your hard drive from www.waltersanford .com/insiderinvestingforms. The document can then be opened, edited, and printed using Microsoft Word or another popular word processing application.

(continued)

Stove, Refrigerator, W/D, AC units: _____

_____

Carpets, Drapes, Furnishings: _____

_____

Lease information to be included in this section. File actual legal documents (lease or rental agreements) and maintain old documents.

Downloadable FORM 18.19
Move-Out Cleaning Instructions to Tenant*

Date: _____ Tenant's Name(s): _____

Address: _____

City/State/Zip: _____

Apartment No.: _____ Garage No.: _____

Kitchen:

1. Clean refrigerator, shelves, crisper, under crisper, and under foot guard.

2. Clean cabinets, under sink, tile, exhaust fan, and faucet fixtures.

3. Clean under burners, controls, and burner rings and drip pans.

4. Clean oven outside and inside.

5. Clean, strip, and wax floor.

6. Clean air-conditioning and heating unit closet, where applicable.

Living Room and Dining Room:

1. Clean cupboards, closets, baseboards, doors, drawers, and all woodwork.

2. Clean fireplace where applicable.

3. Clean traverse rods.

Bedrooms:

1. Same as living room and dining room.

2. Vacuum closets, remove clothes hangers, wipe shelves clean. Remove all debris.

Bathroom:

1. Thoroughly clean tub, toilet, toilet tank, vanity bowl, cupboards, mirrors, and woodwork.

2. Clean chrome fixtures throughout, clean exhaust fan.

3. Clean medicine cabinet, inside and outside.

4. Clean tile, shower area, shower doors, and shower door runners.

5. Clean, strip, and wax floor.

---

*Copyright © 2006 by Walter Sanford. To customize this document, download to your hard drive from www.waltersanford.com/insiderinvestingforms. The document can then be opened, edited, and printed using Microsoft Word or another popular word processing application.

(continued)

Garage, Patios, and Garbage Collection Areas:

1. Clean patios and sweep and clean garbage collection area.

2. Sweep garage floor; carry away all refuse. Clean storage compartments.

Additional Areas to Clean:

1. All carpets and drapes must be commercially cleaned and rehung. Receipts for costs of cleaning must be submitted to Landlord.

2. Finger marks or smudges must be cleaned off light and outlet switches, and all woodwork.

3. All windows must be washed, windowsills cleaned, and screens washed or cleaned. (Do not remove screens.)

Keys must be surrendered during business hours 9 a.m. to 5 p.m. on last day of tenancy, by delivering or mailing keys to Landlord. Envelope must be postmarked last day of tenancy. Otherwise, rent will be charged until keys and garage door openers are received. Please provide forwarding contact information.

Downloadable FORM 18.20
Notice to Enter Dwelling*

To: _____

Address: _____

City: _____ ST: _____ Zip: _____

On _____, between the hours of _____ and

_____ it will be necessary for the owner and/or agent to enter your dwelling

unit for the following reasons:

_____   1. To make necessary or agreed repairs, decorations, alterations, or
            improvements.

_____   2. Supply necessary or agreed services.

_____   3. Exhibit the dwelling unit to prospective or actual purchasers.

_____   4. To exhibit the dwelling to prospective lenders.

_____   5. To exhibit the dwelling unit to prospective tenants.

_____   6. To exhibit the dwelling unit to workmen or contractors.

_____   7. Pursuant to court order.

_____   8. Inspect, test, repair, or maintain smoke detectors.

If you have changed the locks, please provide us with a key, or you will be charged
for a locksmith to gain access per the above request.

_____   _____
            Date   Owner/Agent

*Copyright © 2006 by Walter Sanford. To customize this document, download to your hard drive from www.waltersanford.com/insiderinvestingforms. The document can then be opened, edited, and printed using Microsoft Word or another popular word processing application.

Downloadable FORM 18.21
Resident's Maintenance Repair Request*

Date: _____

Address: _____

_____

Resident's Name: _____

Phone (H): _____ Phone (W): _____

E-mail: _____

Problem: _____

_____

_____

_____

_____

Comments (including best time to make repairs): _____

_____

_____

_____

_____

_____

I authorize entry into my unit to perform the maintenance or repair requested above, in my absence, unless stated otherwise above.

_____   _____
            Resident   Resident

*Copyright © 2006 by Walter Sanford. To customize this document, download to your hard drive from www.waltersanford .com/insiderinvestingforms. The document can then be opened, edited, and printed using Microsoft Word or another popular word processing application.

For Management Use

Work done: _____

_____

_____

_____

_____

_____

Time spent: _____ hour(s)

Date completed: _____, 20 _____

Unable to complete on: _____, 20 _____

Downloadable FORM 18.22

Time Estimate for Repairs*

Date

Name
Address
City, ST Zip

Name:

Thank you for promptly notifying us of the following problem with our unit:

_____

_____

_____

_____

We expect to have the problem corrected on _____, 20 _____, due to the

following: _____

_____

Sincerely,

Walter Sanford
Sanford Systems

*Copyright © 2006 by Walter Sanford. To customize this document, download to your hard drive from www.waltersanford
.com/insiderinvestingforms. The document can then be opened, edited, and printed using Microsoft Word or another popular word processing application.

Downloadable FORM 18.23
Unit Maintenance Record*

Property: _____ Unit: _____

Drapes					
Date	Action	Occupant	By Whom	Time	Cost

Carpet Floor					
Date	Action	Occupant	By Whom	Time	Cost

*Copyright © 2006 by Walter Sanford. To customize this document, download to your hard drive from www.waltersanford .com/insiderinvestingforms. The document can then be opened, edited, and printed using Microsoft Word or another popular word processing application.

(continued)

Downloadable FORM 18.23   *(Continued)*

Paint					
Date	Action	Occupant	By Whom	Time	Cost
Miscellaneous Repairs					
Date	Action	Occupant	By Whom	Time	Cost

Semiannual Safety and Maintenance Update*

Please complete the following checklist and note any safety or maintenance problems in your unit or on the premises.

Please describe the specific problems and the rooms or areas involved. Here are some examples of the types of things we want to know about: the garage roof leaking, excessive mildew in rear bedroom closet, fuses that blow out frequently, door locks that stick, water temperature too high in a shower, nonworking exhaust fan above stove, smoke alarm malfunctions, peeling paint, and mice in basement. Please point out any potential safety and security problems in the neighborhood and anything you consider a serious nuisance.

Please indicate the approximate date when you first noticed the problem and list any other recommendations or suggestions for improvement.

Please return this form with this month's rent check. Thank you.

Sanford Systems
559 S. Washington Ave. • Kankakee, IL 60901
P: 815.929.9258 • E: walter@waltersanford.com

Name: _____

Address: _____

_____

Please indicate (and explain below) problems with:
Floors and floor coverings
Walls and ceiling
Windows, screens, and doors
Window coverings (drapes, miniblinds, etc.)
Electrical system and light fixtures
Plumbing (sinks, bathtub, shower, or toilet)
Heating or air-conditioning system
Major appliances (stove, oven, dishwasher, refrigerator)
Basement or attic

*Copyright © 2006 by Walter Sanford. To customize this document, download to your hard drive from www.waltersanford.com/insiderinvestingforms. The document can then be opened, edited, and printed using Microsoft Word or another popular word processing application.

(continued)

Locks or security system
Smoke detector
Fireplace
Cupboards, cabinets, and closets
Furnishings (table, bed, mirrors, chairs)
Laundry facilities
Elevator
Stairs and handrails
Hallway and common areas
Garage
Patio, terrace, or deck
Lawn, fences, and grounds
Pool and recreational facilities
Roof, exterior walls, and other structural problems
Driveway and sidewalks
Neighborhood
Nuisances
Other

Specifics of problems: _____

_____

_____

_____

Other Comments: _____

_____

_____

_____

_____   _____
Date   Tenant's Signature

For Management Use

Action/Response: _____

_____

_____

_____

_____   _____
Date   Owner/Manager

Downloadable FORM 18.25
Move-In/Move-Out Inspection Checklist*

Street Address	Unit No.		City	State	Zip Code

Tenant	Landlord/Agent	Move-in Date

Inspection date: In: _____   Out: _____

Code:

Location   **Condition**

T	Top	B	Bottom		DI	Dirty	SC	Scratch	LE	Leak	BO	Bulb Out
L	Left	R	Right		SP	Spot	WO	Worn	RU	Rust	NA	Nail
M	Mid	F	Front		ST	Stain	TR	Tear	CO	Corr.	NW	Not Working
BA	Back	E	Edge		BU	Burn	CR	Crack	RM	R/Mod	MI	Missing
C	Corner	S	Side		ME	Melt	CU	Cut	LO	Loose	MA	Major
					HO	Hole	BK	Break	WO	Worn	MR	Minor

Rooms:

EN Entry (Hall)   LR Living   DR Dining   BR Bed   BA Bath   CL Closet

Room	Feature/Article	Condition (Move-In)	Repairs Needed or Comments	Condition (Move-Out)	Initial Repairs by Landlord/Tenant

*Copyright © 2006 by Walter Sanford. To customize this document, download to your hard drive from www.waltersanford .com/insiderinvestingforms. The document can then be opened, edited, and printed using Microsoft Word or another popular word processing application.

The move-in or move-out inspection on this and attached pages represents a true record of the rental unit's contents and our best opinion of its condition at the time of inspection.

Move-in Inspection:

Tenant: _____ Landlord/Agent: _____ Date: _____

Move-out Inspection:

Tenant: _____ Landlord/Agent: _____ Date: _____

	Move-In Inspection		**Move-Out Inspection**		
Article	Location Code	Condition Code	Location Code	Condition Code	Comments (Repairs)

Instructions: Inspect each article of furniture and accessories in rental unit. Note the condition and location. Include any special problems or repairs to be made in the comment section.

(continued)

Move-in Inspection:

Tenant: _____ Landlord/Agent: _____ Date: _____

Move-out Inspection:

Tenant: _____ Landlord/Agent: _____ Date: _____

Property Inspection Report*

Date/Time: _____

Tenant Name: _____

Owner's Name: _____

Unit's Address: _____

City, State, and Zip: _____

Initial Inspection	Re-Inspection	Final Inspection
Occupied	Vacant	

Entry

Doors: _____

Walls: _____

Ceiling: _____

Floor: _____

Light Fixture: _____

Misc: _____

Misc: _____

Misc: _____

Living Room

Doors: _____

Walls: _____

Ceiling: _____

Floor: _____

Light Fixture: _____

Closet: _____

Windows: _____

Fireplace: _____

Dining Room

Doors: _____

Walls: _____

Ceiling: _____

Floor: _____

Light Fixture: _____

Windows: _____

Misc: _____

Misc: _____

Misc: _____

Den

Doors: _____

Walls: _____

Ceiling: _____

Floor: _____

Light Fixture: _____

Windows: _____

Closet: _____

Fireplace: _____

Bar: _____

---

*Copyright © 2006 by Walter Sanford. To customize this document, download to your hard drive from www.waltersanford.com/insiderinvestingforms. The document can then be opened, edited, and printed using Microsoft Word or another popular word processing application.

(continued)

Bathroom 1

Doors: _____

Walls: _____

Ceiling: _____

Floor: _____

Light Fixture: _____

Toilet: _____

Basin: _____

Tub: _____

Shower: _____

Cabinets: _____

Linen Storage: _____

Formica Tile: _____

Overhead Heater: _____

Bathroom 2

Doors: _____

Walls: _____

Ceiling: _____

Floor: _____

Light Fixture: _____

Toilet: _____

Basin: _____

Tub: _____

Shower: _____

Cabinets: _____

Linen Storage: _____

Formica Tile: _____

Overhead Heater: _____

Bedroom 1

Doors: _____

Walls: _____

Ceiling: _____

Floor: _____

Light Fixture: _____

Windows: _____

Closet: _____

Bedroom 2

Doors: _____

Walls: _____

Ceiling: _____

Floor: _____

Light Fixture: _____

Windows: _____

Closet: _____

Bedroom 3

Doors: _____

Walls: _____

Ceiling: _____

Floor: _____

Light Fixture: _____

Windows: _____

Closet: _____

Bedroom 4

Doors: _____

Walls: _____

Ceiling: _____

Floor: _____

Light Fixture: _____

Windows: _____

Closet: _____

Utility Room

Doors: _____

Walls: _____

Ceiling: _____

Floor: _____

Closet: _____

Windows: _____

Misc: _____

Misc: _____

Misc: _____

Other

Air Conditioning: _____

Washing Machine: _____

Dryer: _____

Heating: _____

Water Heater: _____

Front Door Lock: _____

Back Door Lock: _____

Stairs: _____

Misc: _____

Exterior

Porch: _____

Garage Door: _____

Stairs: _____

Roof: _____

Driveway: _____

Front Yard: _____

Exterior, cont'd.

Back Yard: _____

Fence: _____

Screen Doors: _____

Exterior Doors: _____

Foundation: _____

Patio: _____

Downloadable FORM 18.27
Unit Ledger Card*

Unit Number: _____   Property: _____

Date	Occupant	Rent Period Mo./Yr. From	To	Payment Credited To: _____ Miscellaneous Rent	Security Deposit	Amount	Description	Total Amount Received	Remarks

*Copyright © 2006 by Walter Sanford. To customize this document, download to your hard drive from www.waltersanford .com/insiderinvestingforms. The document can then be opened, edited, and printed using Microsoft Word or another popular word processing application.

Downloadable FORM 18.28
Tenant Ledger Card*

Property: _____ Unit _____

Name: _____ Phone: _____

E-mail: _____

Employed by: _____ Phone: _____

In case of emergency contact: _____ Phone: _____

Lease Term: From: _____ To: _____

Monthly Rent Unit _____ $_____

               Unit _____ $_____

               Unit _____ $_____

               Total $_____

Date	Rent Period Month/Year		Payment Credited					Remarks
	From	To	Total Amount	Security Deposit	Rent	Late Charge	Other	

*Copyright © 2006 by Walter Sanford. To customize this document, download to your hard drive from www.waltersanford .com/insiderinvestingforms. The document can then be opened, edited, and printed using Microsoft Word or another popular word processing application.

Downloadable FORM 18.29
Monthly Rent Delinquency Report*

Property: _____

Date: _____ Date Rent Due: _____

Address	Occupant	Amount Due	Move-in Date	Date of Delinquency Notice	Times Delinquent

Total Occupants Delinquent: _____ Total Amount Delinquent: $_____

Prepared by: _____

*Copyright © 2006 by Walter Sanford. To customize this document, download to your hard drive from www.waltersanford .com/insiderinvestingforms. The document can then be opened, edited, and printed using Microsoft Word or another popular word processing application.

Downloadable FORM 18.30
Agreement for Partial Rent Payments*

_____, Owner and

_____, Tenant agree

on the rent due as follows: _____

1. Tenant has paid $_____ on _____,

   20 _____, which was due on _____, 20 _____.

2. Owner agrees to accept the remainder of the rent and late charge totaling

   $_____ on or before _____, 20 _____

   and to hold off on any legal proceeding to evict Tenant until the next day after the

   above date should total payment not be made.

_____	_____
Date	Tenant

_____	_____
Date	Owner

*Copyright © 2006 by Walter Sanford. To customize this document, download to your hard drive from www.waltersanford.com/insiderinvestingforms. The document can then be opened, edited, and printed using Microsoft Word or another popular word processing application.

Downloadable FORM 18.31
Residential Questionnaire*

A few moments of your time in completing this questionnaire can be of great value to us in seeing that we provide the services expected by you and in helping us make your home one that we can all be proud of.

Property Address: _____

Unit number (optional): _____   Number living in unit: _____

Type of unit: _____

Length of time in current apartment: _____

Length of time in this apartment community: _____

Length of time you plan to live in an apartment before purchasing a home or condominium:

_____

Your Name: _____   Date: _____

Contact Information: _____

Please indicate your opinion by making checks in the appropriate columns:

General Maintenance and Upkeep:	Far Below Average	Slightly Below Average	Average	Slightly Above Average	Far Above Average
Your home	❏	❏	❏	❏	❏
Lawns and landscaping	❏	❏	❏	❏	❏
Walkways	❏	❏	❏	❏	❏
Exterior of building	❏	❏	❏	❏	❏
Hallways and entrance ways	❏	❏	❏	❏	❏
Recreational facilities	❏	❏	❏	❏	❏
Laundry rooms	❏	❏	❏	❏	❏
Storage rooms	❏	❏	❏	❏	❏

_____

_____

Other comments: _____

*Copyright © 2006 by Walter Sanford. To customize this document, download to your hard drive from www.waltersanford .com/insiderinvestingforms. The document can then be opened, edited, and printed using Microsoft Word or another popular word processing application.

Downloadable FORM 18.31   *(Continued)*

	Far Below Average	Slightly Below Average	Average	Slightly Above Average	Far Above Average
Personnel:					
On-site manager	❏	❏	❏	❏	❏
Courteous	❏	❏	❏	❏	❏
Efficient	❏	❏	❏	❏	❏
Available when needed	❏	❏	❏	❏	❏
Appearance	❏	❏	❏	❏	❏

Other comments: _____

	Far Below Average	Slightly Below Average	Average	Slightly Above Average	Far Above Average
Other on-site personnel	❏	❏	❏	❏	❏
Courteous	❏	❏	❏	❏	❏
Efficient	❏	❏	❏	❏	❏
Available when needed	❏	❏	❏	❏	❏
Appearance	❏	❏	❏	❏	❏

Other comments: _____

	Far Below Average	Slightly Below Average	Average	Slightly Above Average	Far Above Average
Your Home:					
Floor plan	❏	❏	❏	❏	❏
Size of rooms	❏	❏	❏	❏	❏
Closet space	❏	❏	❏	❏	❏
Carpet/floors	❏	❏	❏	❏	❏
Bath(s)	❏	❏	❏	❏	❏
Kitchen	❏	❏	❏	❏	❏
Appliances	❏	❏	❏	❏	❏
Light Fixtures	❏	❏	❏	❏	❏

_____

_____

Other comments: _____

(continued)

Downloadable FORM 18.31   *(Continued)*

	Far Below Average	Slightly Below Average	Average	Slightly Above Average	Far Above Average
The Property:					
Physical appearance	❑	❑	❑	❑	❑
General construction	❑	❑	❑	❑	❑
Parking facilities	❑	❑	❑	❑	❑
Additional storage	❑	❑	❑	❑	❑
Recreational facilities	❑	❑	❑	❑	❑

Other comments: _____

Have your service requests been handled:

Promptly: Yes   No   Efficiently: Yes   No   Gone unanswered: Yes   No

Other comments: _____

_____

Would you live in another property managed by:

Your current on-site manager?   Yes   No

The current management company?   Yes   No

If not, why? _____

Would you recommend this property to your friends?   Yes   No

If not, why?_____

Would you be interested in more planned social activities in your apartment community, if

applicable?   Yes   No

If yes, what kinds of activities: _____

Why did you move to this community:

Best value: _____

Convenience: _____

Social amenities: _____

Plan or design: _____

Other (please specify): _____

Downloadable FORM 18.31   *(Continued)*

General Information:

Did you first visit this property as a result on an advertisement?   Yes   No

If yes, which one? _____

Which local newspaper do you read regularly? _____

What radio station do you listen to regularly? _____

How much time do you spend listening to the radio each day? _____

What television station do you watch regularly? _____

What is your favorite program? _____

What are your favorite viewing hours? _____

What rental Internet sites do you visit? _____

Additional comments: _____

_____

_____

_____

_____

_____

Thank you very much for spending the time to complete this questionnaire. We plan to use the suggestions of our residents to continually improve our properties.

Downloadable FORM 18.32

Warning Notice (Complaints from Neighborhood/Residents)*

Date: _____

Memorandum from Owner/Manager

To:_____, Resident(s) of Property at:

_____

Re: Complaints from neighbors/other residents

Several of your neighbors have complained to the management regarding the following disturbance or condition:

_____

_____

_____

Approximate date of occurrence: _____. It is very important to the management that our residents be able to enjoy the peace and quiet of their homes. Disturbing or affecting neighbors is a violation of the terms of your lease/rental agreement. You are requested to take the following corrective action:

_____

_____

If you have any questions please contact _____ at

_____.

Sincerely,

Owner/Manager

*Copyright © 2006 by Walter Sanford. To customize this document, download to your hard drive from www.waltersanford .com/insiderinvestingforms. The document can then be opened, edited, and printed using Microsoft Word or another popular word processing application.

Downloadable FORM 18.33
Move-Out Letter*

Date

Name
Address
City, ST Zip

Name:

We hope you have enjoyed living here. I hope that we can be of service to you in your future real estate transactions. Remember, we have many financial benefits for you including referral fees, if you find us a tenant as great as you, assistance toward your down payment if you buy from us, and secret properties that no one else will ever show you!

Before vacating, be sure to request and complete our move out instruction checklist.

Once you have cleaned your unit and removed all your belongings, contact me at
_____ to arrange for a walk-through inspection and to return the keys and garage door openers.

Also, please provide a forwarding address where we may mail your security deposit, less any lawful deductions for the cost of necessary cleaning and repairs of damage in excess of ordinary wear and tear and any past-due rent. We will return your deposit balance and an itemization of any charges, within two weeks after you move out.

We appreciated being your landlord and we would like to now be your advisor in buying and selling real estate. Please call me for a free consultation.

If you have any questions, please contact me at 815.929.9258.

Sincerely,

Walter Sanford
Sanford Systems

*Copyright © 2006 by Walter Sanford. To customize this document, download to your hard drive from www.waltersanford.com/insiderinvestingforms. The document can then be opened, edited, and printed using Microsoft Word or another popular word processing application.

Downloadable FORM 18.34
Exit Interview*

We are sorry to learn that you are leaving. We are living in a mobile society and there can be many reasons for such a move, but we would like to know if there has been anything about your occupancy with us that has prompted this decision. We would appreciate your taking a moment to respond to the questions below and returning your answers in the stamped, self-addressed envelope or complete online at www.waltersanford.com. It is our goal to be an asset and resource to your real estate making decisions.

1. Have you been pleased with the general appearance of the grounds, walks, and other facilities and the manner in which they have been maintained?

   Please specify: _____

   _____

   _____

2. Have you been treated courteously and fairly by the on-site manager? Has the manager been available when needed?

   Please specify: _____

   _____

   _____

3. Is there anything that we might have done to encourage you to continue as a resident in our apartment community?

   Please specify: _____

   _____

   _____

4. Reason for leaving (check one or more):

   Moving to a larger apartment ❑

   Moving to a smaller apartment ❑

   Moving to a newer apartment ❑

   Moving to an older apartment ❑

   Purchasing a home ❑

   Dissatisfied with management ❑

   Moving out of area ❑

   Other: _____ ❑

*Copyright © 2006 by Walter Sanford. To customize this document, download to your hard drive from www.waltersanford .com/insiderinvestingforms. The document can then be opened, edited, and printed using Microsoft Word or another popular word processing application.

5. Any other comments or suggestions as to how your stay with us could have been made more pleasant?

    Please specify: _____

    _____

    _____

6. If you were to buy a new home, could you tell us a little about how it would look?

    Please specify: _____

    _____

    _____

7. Do you currently know of any other tenants who might want to move into any of

    our properties?   ❏ Yes   ❏ No

    Could we have permission to call them and use you as a reference?

    Their names: _____

    _____

    _____

    Phone: _____ E-mail: _____

8. Would you like to know how easy it is to buy and qualify for no-money-down

    loans?   ❏ Yes   ❏ No

Your Name: _____

Your Signature: _____ Date: _____

Property Address: _____

New Home Phone: _____ Business Phone: _____

Downloadable FORM 18.35
Move-Out Closing Statement*

Resident's name: _____

Address of premises: _____

Date of tenancy began: _____ Date vacating: _____

Date keys and openers turned in: _____ , 20 _____

Forwarding address: _____

City/State/Zip: _____

Phone: _____ Phone: _____ E-mail: _____

Submitted by: _____ Date: _____

Credit	Amount
Rent Credit: Days @ $ _____ Per Day	$
Other	$
Total Credits	$
Charges—See receipts and explanation on reverse	Amount
Cleaning _____	$
Unpaid Late Charges _____	$
Damage _____	$
Unpaid Utilities _____	$
Rent Due: $_____ days @ $_____ per day	$
Total Charges	$
Balance due residents within 14 days of redelivery of keys and openers	$
Other:	$
Balance due Owners within 14 Days	$

*Copyright © 2006 by Walter Sanford. To customize this document, download to your hard drive from www.waltersanford.com/insiderinvestingforms. The document can then be opened, edited, and printed using Microsoft Word or another popular word processing application.

CHAPTER 19

Your Insider Advantages as a Seller

It is time to talk about a subject that is very unappealing to me—selling real estate equity. The question is "Have you ever sold one of your investment properties?" The honest answer is "Well, yeah." More than once, I have bought a property that turned out not to be what I thought it was. It seemed to be haunted whenever I tried to rent it, the rental gains came slowly, or the neighborhood was not as desirable as it had appeared. Sometimes I sold a property because I found a faster moving vehicle, was short of funds, and had a ready buyer—or was just stupid! And I have regretted those sales.

Even though I did everything possible to not sell a property, the inevitable sale occasionally happened, and then I was glad that I was an insider. Being a real estate broker and selling your own property can be fraught with problems, but if you are fair and disclose *all* aspects of the property, there is no reason you cannot sell it effectively. You will have several insider advantages:

- It is an automatic listing, where you will earn your 3 percent or more commission and acquire more buyers and sellers from marketing it.
- You may not have to list the property to sell it. Since you are the negotiator between buyers and sellers and meet buyers every day, you may find a person in need of a quick purchase that matches a property in your secret inventory of personal ownership. Not only are you a hero for meeting the buyer's needs despite the time constraint, but you are also making a market value sale without having to pay a commission to a cooperating agent.
- Since you have been managing the property that you are selling, acquiring a management contract from your buyers is profitable. This is because the majority of management costs for properties occur in the start-up months and you have already

covered those costs. You are extending over an already effective system of management for your buyer.

• Listing a property gives you several advantages—advertising attracts more buyers, notifies other owners in the neighborhood for additional opportunities, and allows you to approach your tenants as potential buyers. This has worked best for me when the property in question had been misused, with one component diverted to commercial use. I owned a property in Long Beach that had four units and a dental office. The dentist chased me for years trying to buy the property. Since his business and clientele were already established, he was prepared to pay top dollar for the property.

Being an insider with owned inventory is an outstanding position for achieving a sale; even though a sale is certainly not my goal.

At some point, someone is going to sell your real estate—if not you, then possibly your heirs. I have placed all my real estate in trusts to minimize probate cost (see a trust attorney for details), but it is incumbent on me to help you get your property ready for sale, even though you have no intention of selling it.

I keep my selling checklist (Form 19.1) at the back of my Property Summary Folder (see Chapter 16). By providing the information on the form, you can direct your heirs or trustees in taking the necessary steps to sell the property.

Reasons Insiders Should Not Sell

Selling immediately stops your positive incoming cash flow. It stops the equity paydown and may force you to obtain replacement financing for a new property at higher rates. It incurs closing costs, and in many cases, it causes the IRS to tax you. The fastest way to avoid these negatives is to maintain due diligence in your real estate brokerage business: Use our systems to make a profit and run your building so it does not drive you crazy. This strategy will allow you to happily acquire and keep real estate. The snowball effect will soon carry you to financial independence. Insiders who keep their real estate finish first!

Selling Checklist*

Property Address: _____

Date Purchased: _____ Date Sold: _____

Does the sale of this property qualify for long-term tax treatment? _____

    Selling Information: Price: $_____

                         Down payment received: $_____

                         Balance due: $_____

Name of Buyer: _____

Has buyer obtained insurance?   Yes   No   (or enclose proper documents)

Financing Terms: _____

    New insurance agent: _____

    Phone No.: _____ Policy No.: _____

Is the new buyer assuming any loans: Yes   No

Information on assumptions: _____

_____

_____

Wraparound created?   Yes   No

State Terms: _____

_____

_____

Is any part of the down payment being financed by you? If so, explain terms:

_____

Other Information: _____

_____

_____

*Copyright © 2006 by Walter Sanford. To customize this document, download to your hard drive from www.waltersanford .com/insiderinvestingforms. The document can then be opened, edited, and printed using Microsoft Word or another popular word processing application.

(continued)

Are the payments being collected and/or dispersed by a different company?   Yes   No

If yes, fill out the following information:

Company name: _____

Address: _____

Terms of Arrangement: _____

Does this sale qualify for Section 1031 tax treatment?   Yes   No

If so, enclose the proper exchange documents and tax forms.

List here all documents for selling this property that are included in this file:

1. _____

2. _____

3. _____

4. _____

Closing costs paid: _____

Instructions for executor in case of death or disability: _____

_____

_____

Were partners added to the ownership of this property before disposition? _____

Explain: _____

_____

_____

_____

_____

Were loans taken out or was the property refinanced before disposition?

Explain: _____

_____

_____

_____

_____

What are the tax implications of selling? _____

_____

_____

What are the reasons for *not* selling? _____

_____

_____

CHAPTER 20

Other Insider Profits

Not all insider benefits have to do with the acquisition of investment real estate and basic dealings with buyers, sellers, and tenants; other profitable situations come from your insider status.

One of the most satisfying aspects is your opportunity to meet people and share in the profits from partnerships, joint ventures, and promissory notes that are created to transfer real estate. I used my real estate systems to develop more clients, and my favorite clients were builders. I would find all the builders, contractors, engineers, and architects who worked and produced buildings in my local area. I developed a letter for this database offering these people free advertising on my web site for promoting themselves, their resumes, and their projects.

I also had a form for potential buyers who wanted to build or design a new home, and I gave these leads to the builders. I offered free advice on floor plans and elevations, pointing out changes that would make properties more salable. I sent builders multiple listing service (MLS) access, to every lot, land, and acreage listing on a weekly basis, so they would be aware of all new land inventory. I gave them access to all my team members, offering the best in financing, home inspections, title, insurance, and any other relationships that I had developed in my real estate business. I offered them 20 percent referral fees on any resale transaction they generated from the sale of their new properties.

Most new properties involve a buyer who already owns a piece of real estate and needs to sell it. I was effective in selling the downleg in this situation and making a commission, while the builder who was instrumental in my receiving the listing received an additional income source by helping the buyer achieve liquidity that would enable closing on the builder's project.

I also offered a reinvested commission: If the builder or any of the affiliated industries bought land from me and I earned a commission from that sale, I would apply my commission toward the down payment of the land in return for a limited partnership in the project. I used my insider status not only to appeal to the builders but also to become a partner with many of them. The partnership often became a friendship; in many cases, I was chosen to list the property when it was completed and was offered the first chance at other opportunities in the area. These relationships and opportunities would not be available to ordinary investors without a real estate license.

As an insider, I also could discuss the purchase or sale of promissory notes secured by real estate. In many real estate transactions, a note is produced as a seller carryback, in possibly a second or third position. Often the people who carry these notes really do not want to carry paper, but have to sell the property. These notes, which can be purchased at less than face value, allow the owner to become *liquid,* and allow you to become the new owner of the promissory note at a favorable yield. These transactions require a special skill set; however, if there is enough equity in the property, if the payer on the note has a good financial statement, and if you receive financial information on that payer—you can be confident that the note will be profitable. If there is a default, you will receive a piece of real estate where the equity will be worth more than the value of the note.

When you have an opportunity to buy a note with enough equity in the property to protect you and the payer seems to be solid, then all that is necessary is to have someone help you figure out how much of a discount is necessary to produce the yield you are looking for. If a $50,000 note is payable at 9 percent interest monthly, how much would the discount have to be to present a 20 percent yield? These calculations are easily found on current real estate software. If you do not know how to figure the net present value of money, you might want to take a lesson from a Certified Commercial Investment Member (CCIM) or from another real estate agent who can explain the concept and equations.

At different points in my career, I also have made insider profits from ancillary businesses. Top real estate agents often move laterally into owning real estate offices or create income flows from mortgage, escrow, or title businesses. These ancillary businesses are available to you as additional sources of profit in the business that you already know and love. Keep your eyes open for all the opportunities of your insider status.

CHAPTER 21

Do You Have What It Takes to Be an Inside Investor?

If you make a net profit from your brokerage business and consider real estate for yourself before you pass it on to a client, you have what it takes! Developing a net profit in the real estate brokerage business is something that Sanford Systems and Strategies has been teaching for the past 15 years. I have used my successes and those of my peers to develop an easy-to-follow plan—while still having a life. There are nine rules in our business plan:

1. We control the listings, and we are experts in seller lead generation.

2. We can present a better client-satisfying listing presentation than anyone else in our community, allowing us to take listings at the right price.

3. We know how to deal with the buyers generated from our listings to maximize our effectiveness. We turn down and refer many buyers who do not cooperate with systems put in place for their own good.

4. We develop systems and checklists that allow us to be consistent in the service that we give, and we never forget the things that have made us successful.

5. We put together a team of affiliates who have generated a large income from our business and who are ready, willing, and able to provide services to our clients and to us, including third-party endorsement letters and joint lead generation systems.

6. We consistently maintain amazing relationships with our clients by personally staying in touch with them. We always ask them if they know of any referral or repeat business that we can work on and whether they will consider investment property to increase their yield on their real estate experiences.

7. We provide and implement profitable technology in our offices that increases our clients' satisfaction while decreasing the time spent on this business and increasing our net bottom line.

8. We learn how to be our own best client by considering projects for ourselves before turning them over to our clients, and we make sure that these offerings meet specific real estate goals that we set out in advance.

9. We try to rule our whole operations within the confines of our six "F" words: *family, fun, faith, fitness, friends,* and personal *finances.* We never let the business overtake these "F" words, because it would create an imbalance and make the wheels come off our real estate wagon.

If you follow these rules, your real estate brokerage business will point you in the direction of net income and great real estate investments. If you have made strides in becoming a profitable real estate agent or broker, moving into the real estate investment arena will be easy. You have the money and the leads, so get ready to take that step by reflecting on the following considerations.

Many real estate agents are so hung up on adding listings or sales to the production board in the office that they overlook great personal investment opportunities. It is not until you realize that the greatest profits come from real estate investing that you will start thinking about these projects for yourself.

Very few agents are financially independent solely from commissions. When you discover that real estate investing can accomplish your financial goals, you will start setting aside small percentages of your closed commission dollars and wiring them to a money market fund. This will provide the impetus for a down payment.

Once you obtain a down payment, you will start looking at projects that meet conservative rules for investment. You will pay more attention to your personal FICO scores so that you can obtain financing. You will look at free-and-clear properties with enthusiasm as you consider seller-carryback financing. You will filter everything through your criteria as an investor instead of as a broker.

When you wake up in the morning, your goals for buying real estate will provide you with motivation and help you avoid burnout. This book gives you the knowledge and fosters your determination to make the actions happen.

Sit down right now and discuss with your inner self the goals that you must achieve to have a perfect life. You will find that many of these goals are dependent on increasing your equity, or net worth. Financial success can cure fear of failure and provide proof of self-worth. If others have said that you do not have what it takes, you will prove them wrong. Success will provide public notoriety, prestige, a carefree lifestyle, freedom, and enough money to help others and to acquire material comforts such as vacation properties, automobiles, and toys.

It is important to monitor yourself frequently and make certain that you are on the path necessary to achieve your success. I always knew that I wanted "100 doors"—100 units. For me, once these properties are free and clear, they will give me enough net income to live the lifestyle that I have designed. I have reached this goal three times in my life. Two of those times I lost the majority of my properties by being stupid. I messed up the balance in my life and the wheels came off. As you are acquiring your wealth by being a great real estate agent and your own best client, check often to make certain that your goals are in alignment with your core beliefs—family, fun, faith, fitness, friends, and personal finances.

This book will not be the end of your education to become your own best client and insider investor, but it describes the majority of the brush strokes that you must master. Along with having goals for purchases and a great real estate brokerage business, you need to put yourself in position for success. Do you have an area where you can work six to eight hours a day without interruption, surrounded by reminders of your goals and by all the business equipment necessary to effectively conduct transactions, serve your clients, and keep your files straight? Do not skimp on the investment in your business. Before you invest in real estate, you should invest in the necessary tools to operate your real estate brokerage efficiently.

Also, take the time to check your moral and ethical standards. Early in your career, it is easy to make mistakes. I promise you that taking shortcuts on transactions will always come back to bite you in the rear! Whenever you take advantage of a client, the misdeed will come back to haunt you. Learn from the mistakes of thousands of people before you and just do not do it. If you need to lie, exaggerate, or hide something about a transaction, just cancel that transaction. There is no shame in walking away from a transaction that might hurt someone. There is shame if you meet your goals by stealing from someone else. I am proud to say that I have sought only win-win transactions that would meet the needs of the buyer and seller as well as my own goals. I fully disclosed my intentions to clients up front. Whether I was representing them on a purchase, a sale, or was actually buying the properties, my clients were never surprised. I have said this before: Your return on investment or the commission you make is not worth bending the rules. If your clients trust you, they will confide their needs and desires. This will allow you to explore their goals and create plans to achieve them. Sometimes their goals facilitate yours.

In achieving a client's goals, you will often work on one side of a transaction. The more close relationships you have in this business, the better chance you have of being involved in transactions. This will come from offering the finest service and being willing to go the extra mile in your real estate business. These contacts will turn into further business and more referrals as your database grows. You will find that you have a large group of people who might consider investing with you in a partnership, buying from you, or selling to you. These relationships can provide a never-ending source of future business.

You need to know what good transactions look like. Throughout this book, I have tried to describe them as simply as possible. If you can find a property requiring 10 percent down or more that breaks even with a 40 percent expense factor; if it is in a mediocre to good area; and if it is within driving distance and has long-term, fixed financing—then it should be fairly easy to reach a decision. Remember, *analysis paralysis* happens! If you do not have a clear sense of what makes a great property, you will always be in the brokerage business . . . working. To hesitate means that someone who is more experienced will pick up the property first. But don't worry too much, being an insider means there are more where that came from!

As you achieve your success in the brokerage business and gain numerous properties to rent, you will find that there are many other job openings in the amazing real estate field. You might move into mortgages, title, escrow, insurance, or my favorite—management. Additional flows of income are available with small horizontal moves. We add to them the possibility of buying and selling notes. The opportunity of becoming wealthy as an insider in this business is unlimited. Everything that you do will turn around and add to your listing and selling business just as your listing and selling business adds to your investing business.

Over the years, you may find many shortcuts in real estate operations. You will hear of "no money down" transactions, but in almost all these transactions, the buyer has had to give up something—price, location, terms, or conditions. Then you will hear about alternative downs that create the same problems. You will hear about other ways in which you can make income on the backs of other people, such as lease options, but usually someone is unhappy in a lease option—the person who is going to lose the option money by not closing the sale or the person who is going to sell the property at the option amount in a market that has risen substantially.

Whenever you have a loser in a situation, it is difficult to feel good about the overall transaction. You will hear a lot about *flipping* (quickly turning over a property for sale) and I have done quite a few flips in my life. In almost any flip, you are betting that after purchase you will be able to sell the property. What happens after the refurbishment and you are suddenly in a different real estate market at higher interest rates? Your short-term property does not meet any of your parameters for long-term hold. People who make money in flips always make it on the upswing, but what about the transitional market or downmarket? I have seen people lose fortunes speculating toward the flip. I make certain that I can hold on long term if the property does not get flipped and sold.

I am conservative because I am trying to provide a long-term method for building wealth, not a short-term solution that is dependent on a highly inflated real estate appreciation market or "greater fool theory." I love that some loans are assignable or assumable. Wrapping the loan for a higher yield on the sale is great, but many times the underlying loan is not assumable. Therefore, in a high-interest rate market, the banks come along and want to call the loan after a non-disclosed sale! Beware of investing gurus with solutions that seem too easy or too good to be true. Learn from the mistakes of the past, and if the banks do not allow an assumption of a loan, do not illegally assume it.

Most real estate problems can be cured if you follow the well-known rules of top real estate agents. You have helped many clients change their financial future by the investments you have provided. Now all you need to do is be as responsible to yourself as you have been for clients.

Through your business, you are going to be finding buyers, sellers, and tenants. If you treat these people with courtesy and integrity, they will send you many other buyers, sellers, and tenants. Make certain that you always take care of these people because they are the heart of any real estate operation.

Top agents understand the concept of having cash or cash equivalents. These agents can weather unexpected real estate hiccups. Sometimes a transaction comes along that needs a large influx of cash but has huge returns. It is always smart to have cash reserves, the ability to borrow against your retirement accounts, or even the option of borrowing against your equity. Be ready for immediate needs of cash.

As you are becoming a mover and shaker in the real estate business and community, you can impress your local banker by taking the necessary steps that will allow the loan officer to make a quick positive decision when you ask for a $200,000 signature line of credit. Many times, the primary reason I could overcome the buying competition at a foreclosure or tax sale was that I could present a cashier's check within a few hours or days.

Building your ability to borrow on the short term and always having an exact plan (with backup plans) to pay it back are extremely important factors when acquiring real estate.

When you become a successful real estate agent who serves clients and also puts together investments, one of your greatest joys will be helping your numerous clients achieve their goals while developing your personal investing program. A net worth statement that grows every year is what you will leave as an annuity to your family and church. It is a satisfying outcome in a challenging business.

I am excited about moving you to the next level of real estate and taking you from being a learner to being a *do-er*. In this book, we have laid out the plan and the path. Start walking. . . .

Notes—Insights, Ideas, Actions to Take	Page #
Strategy—Planning for Success	Page #
Tactics—Ways to Achieve Success	Page #

First Step:	Page #

If you have an event where real estate agents or loan officers congregate, fax this completed form to get a $200 value FREE Walter Sanford System!

To send us your request, please fill in the following and choose how you'd like us to respond.

1. Approximate Date of Event(s), just the month would be fine:

   _____   _____

2. Approximate Number in Attendance for the Speaking Event:

   _____

3. Walter's Attendance May Be Needed:

   ☐ Full Day   ☐ Half Day

   ☐ Multiple Days   ☐ Other

4. Who are we having the pleasure of serving? Please fill out the following information:

   Name: _____

   Company/Organization: _____

   Address: _____

   City: _____ ST: _____ Zip: _____

   Office Phone: _____ Home Phone: _____

   Fax: _____ E-mail: _____

5. Do you need any special information? _____

6. How would you like for us to respond?   ☐ Surface Mail   ☐ E-mail

                                             ☐ Fax   ☐ Phone